G☺ TOGETHER

GO TOGETHER

How the Concept of Ubuntu Will Change
How You Live, Work, and Lead

Shola Richards

STERLING ETHOS
New York

STERLING ETHOS
New York

An Imprint of Sterling Publishing Co., Inc.
1166 Avenue of the Americas
New York, NY 10036

ISBN 978-1-4549-2908-6

Distributed in Canada by Sterling Publishing Co., Inc.
c/o Canadian Manda Group, 664 Annette Street
Toronto, Ontario M6S 2C8, Canada
Distributed in the United Kingdom by GMC Distribution Services
Castle Place, 166 High Street, Lewes, East Sussex BN7 1XU, England
Distributed in Australia by NewSouth Books
45 Beach Street, Coogee, NSW 2034, Australia

For information about custom editions, special sales,
and premium and corporate purchases, please contact
Sterling Special Sales at 800-805-5489
or specialsales@sterlingpublishing.com.

Manufactured in the United States of America

2 4 6 8 10 9 7 5 3 1

sterlingpublishing.com

Cover design by David Ter-Avanesyan
Interior design by Christine Heun

To the loves of my life—my wife Amber
and my daughters Kaya and Nia.
In all ways and for the rest of my days,
we will go together. I love you,
and this one is for you.

CONTENTS

INTRODUCTION

If you want to go fast, go alone.
If you want to go far, go together.

—African Proverb

was on a high.

Moments earlier, I had finished delivering a keynote speech at a prestigious northern California university about the critical importance of bringing kindness, positivity, and civility back to the American workplace. That was the key message from my first book, *Making Work Work*, and, ever since its release, I have been asked to share that message in speeches and workshops all over the country. On this particular day, I could not have dreamed for everything to flow together more smoothly— the large audience was enthusiastic and engaged, I delivered my message with as much passion and clarity as I could muster, and, immediately afterward, I was kindly given a long, standing ovation. Yes, I was indeed on a high.

It would not be long before I came crashing back down to earth.

Once all the post-speech handshakes and hugs from the audience were over, I noticed a young woman silently looking at me from the back of the auditorium. I was not sure if she was waiting to speak to me, so as the conference organizer and I walked past her on the way out of the auditorium, I smiled at her. Clearly uncomfortable, she looked down at the floor, avoiding eye contact with me. Initially, I did not think anything of our brief interaction, and the conference organizer and I continued walking toward the front of the building to wait for my ride to the airport. Moments later, the same young woman we had passed in the auditorium rushed over to us with tears in her eyes. There was an urgency on her face that immediately clued me in to the importance of what she was about to say to me.

I was right.

She grabbed my hand, locked her eyes onto mine with a seriousness that shook me to my core, and said the words that helped inspire me to write the book that you are currently reading.

Jordan (not her real name), while still squeezing my left hand, and with her voice trembling, said, "Next week is my twenty-eighth birthday.

And based on the workplace toxicity that I've been dealing with for the past year, I made a decision . . ."

At this point, she paused to look over her shoulder to quickly scan for any eavesdroppers before continuing in a softer tone.

"I made a decision that I was going to end my life before living through another birthday."

Tears flowed from her eyes, and I sensed a relief in her body as those words escaped her lips. It was almost as if speaking those words to another person freed her from the suffocating prison of being alone and misunderstood.

The conference organizer, who was still at my side, stood in wide-eyed disbelief and covered her open mouth with her hand. The two of us briefly exchanged looks that silently communicated, "Did you hear what I just heard?" when the young woman's grip on my hand tightened sharply. It was clear that she had to summon an enormous amount of courage to share these words, and her polite, but firm, hand squeeze was her way to ensure that she had my undivided attention.

"The treatment that I've been receiving at work is destroying my sense of self, my confidence, and, quite honestly, my will to live. *It is like the hatefulness is everywhere.* I said to myself that if I don't receive a sign in the next few days that there is a reason for me to go on, I would take my life the day before my birthday. I reluctantly attended this conference, and once you shared your story, you gave me hope that there are people out there who actually have an interest in changing things in this world. Your words allowed me to regain my power, and, most of all, you spoke to me. Your message was the sign I needed, and, because of you, I will be celebrating my twenty-eighth birthday, and hopefully many more to come. Before you left, I wanted to let you know that you literally saved my life. *I no longer feel alone.* Thank you."

Damn.

I gave Jordan a long hug as she buried her face in my chest and sobbed as if the weight of the world had been lifted from her shoulders. Nothing needed to be said. Even though, on the surface, we could not have been any more different—she was a five-foot-tall, twenty-seven-year-old, blonde-haired, blue-eyed white woman, and I was a six-foot-two, forty-three-year-old black man—in the lobby of that university's student union, we were the same. This was deeper than empathizing with her or feeling her pain. In that moment, *I was her.*

In *Making Work Work*, I opened the book with my story of attempting to end my own life due to the suffocating hopelessness that consumed me as a workplace bullying target. Sharing that very private moment in a very public way with the world was not easy. And as I comforted Jordan, I knew intimately the struggle that was waiting for her if she chose to share her story with anyone else. Sadly, there are no shortage of amateur psychologists out there who would be quick to offer their woefully uninformed diagnosis of Jordan as a weak-minded, spoiled princess who lacks the intestinal fortitude to handle the tough realities of working in the professional world.

Here's the thing, though—this is not a toughness issue. It never has been and it never will be. Workplace bullying is an unrelenting assault on your self-esteem, mental health, and physical well-being—and unless you've been on the wrong side of it, you have no idea how deeply it can affect you. Even worse, it is destroying lives all over the world. If you don't believe me, just type "workplace bullying suicide stories" into a Google search box for an extremely disturbing wake-up call.

Real human lives are at stake here.

Even though I consider myself fully awakened to this harsh reality, what Jordan did for me changed me. After that life-altering moment we shared together, I realized that I needed to widen my focus.

The rabbit hole is *way* deeper than workplace bullying, and it is time I acknowledged that truth.

From the Workplace to the World

Jordan and I ended up talking for a while, and she disclosed more details about the inhuman treatment she was dealing with at work. I like to believe that I have been around the block quite a bit, but what she was dealing with was simply horrific.

Afterward, we traded contact information, vowed to keep in touch (and we have), and I left to fly back home to Los Angeles. My brief high from a well-received keynote speech was eclipsed by a low that left me reeling for months.

My heart broke for Jordan, and, admittedly, I shed tears for her long after our brief meeting. Seven days. That was how narrow the window was for someone, *anyone*, to provide a beautiful soul like Jordan with a reason to continue to stay alive. Seven freaking days. What would have happened if my words had failed to provide her with any meaningful hope? I try not to think about how differently all this could have ended.

What I cannot stop thinking about, even if I wanted to, was one particular sentence that Jordan uttered with equal parts disillusionment and anger.

"It seems like the hatefulness is everywhere."

Everywhere.

This is my new fight. Yes, there are people in workplaces all over the world who are hurting others on a daily basis (and some who take great joy in doing so), but as you and I both know, incivility and hatefulness don't stop once you clock out for the evening.

As I am writing this (and, likely, as you are reading this), we are dealing with divisiveness at an extreme level. It takes many forms. Brown people versus white people. Republicans versus Democrats. Gay people versus straight people. Gun owners versus nongun owners. Climate changers versus climate deniers. Christians versus Muslims versus nonbelievers. Americans versus foreigners. Wall builders versus bridge builders. In many cases, people are so determined to pick sides that they lose sight of the results of their fear-fueled passions.

You have seen the toxic results, too. Hate rallies. Fear and mistrust. Needless violence. Isolation and ostracization. Family members unwilling to break bread together at Thanksgiving in large part because of their perceived differences. And, in extreme cases, people who would rather opt out of this insanity by making the irreversible decision to end their own lives.

We are living in scary times, and unless you don't care about any of this (which I will assume is not the case because you are reading this book), I am going to ask you to play an active role in reversing this troubling trend.

Or, more specifically, I need you to save the world.

That's a big ask, I know. Don't worry, I will be there with you every step of the way. Let's talk about how we're going to do this.

Together.

When We Go Together

A few years ago, I heard an African proverb that changed my life.

"If you want to go fast, go alone. If you want to go far, go together."

In a world that often values speed over meaningful results, it is tempting to think that we can heal these age-old wounds of divisiveness with a quick fix, a shortcut, or a clever hack that one of your buddies shared on your Facebook wall. Far worse than all that, though, is the belief that we can resolve these issues alone. The reality is that throughout history there has never been a problem of any significance that was solved alone. Consider this: Do you really think that you have the ability to solve the divisiveness in our world *by yourself*? If so, I will stop typing and offer you the keyboard to take it from here, because I know that I am completely unequipped to save our world without some help.

No, going alone on this journey is not the answer—believe me, I've tried. The answer to our problems has been under our noses all this time. Thankfully, it doesn't require speed, tireless effort, or rugged individualism.

The solution simply requires us to go together.

Sounds simple, I know—and it is. The challenge is that nothing from this point forward will be easy.

Going together means that you will have to go outside your comfort zone to get the results we seek. Going together means stepping away from people who look like you, think like you, vote like you, and pray like you in order to build new connections with others who are not a part of your tribe. Going together means addressing—and, ideally, healing—the brokenness inside you and me that draws us toward fear instead of toward love. Going together means using every opportunity at your disposal to build bridges instead of walls. Going together means standing courageously against anything or anyone who is actively trying to divide us.

Of course, it would be far easier not to do any of this. It would be much less risky to simply retweet a well-known thought leader's pithy meme from your smartphone, attend a rally for a few hours with a clever handwritten sign, listen to a daily inspirational podcast, or even read books like the one that is currently in your hands, and then walk away with a self-satisfied feeling that your work is done.

The truth is that our work is only beginning. There is so much more that we will need to do together, and my hope is that in the pages that follow, the work that we must do to heal our world will be made clear.

Our path will be illuminated by a single word.

One Word to Change the World

In our conversation together in the student union, Jordan mentioned that there was one word from my speech that had the largest impact on her, and that it would stay with her for the rest of her reclaimed life.

That word is *Ubuntu*.

Ubuntu is often translated to mean, "I am, because we are," and this transcendent African philosophy represents the power of human connectedness, compassion, kindness, and togetherness unlike any single word that I have ever known. It was the central theme of my keynote speech on that day, and it will serve as the central theme of this book as well.

Together, Jordan and I fantasized about a world where this powerful philosophy was ubiquitous.

What if our global mind-set were refocused on the powerful concept of Ubuntu? What if we behaved as if we were literally connected to each other, meaning that there is not a place where I end and you begin? How would that change how we showed up to work each day? How would it change the amount of kindness and respect that we showed to others during our daily life encounters—especially to the people we previously believed were different from us? How would it affect our ability and willingness to lead in a way that would have the deepest positive impact on others?

Besides being desperately needed right now, the reminder that we are all connected in this human journey might be just the way to positively change the world. There is a long road ahead of us, and my hope is that we will make Ubuntu our rallying cry as we walk together on this journey.

Most importantly, though, what Jordan *specifically* said about Ubuntu inspired me to make this powerful word the central theme of this book.

"When I think of the concept of Ubuntu, I no longer feel alone."

I don't know what inspired you to pick up this book. Maybe you are disillusioned by the incivility and divisiveness that is currently gripping our world, and you're looking for some strategies to help reverse this troubling trend. Maybe you are raising young children and need some encouragement that it is possible to leave them with a kinder world than the one they are currently growing up in. Maybe you have grown weary of waiting for leaders in your community, in your workplace and in the political arena to bring us together, so you have decided to courageously step up and do something to bridge the divide. Maybe you are lacking the self-confidence, and self-esteem, and self-belief required to take the first step toward meaningful change. Maybe you sincerely have no idea what to do next. Maybe you are scared and you simply want to know that you are not alone in your fear.

If so, this is the book for you. I am not sure if it helps you to know this, but I am scared, too. However, I am also determined not to let my fear control my actions anymore. What you are about to read are the most personal thoughts I have ever shared publicly, and I hope that by being vulnerable and sharing these thoughts with you, we will form a connection that is stronger than it was before you picked up this book. If you are willing to put in the work to change how we live, work, and lead, the words that follow will serve as your constant reminder that you are not alone on this journey, and you never will be.

To Jordan, to anyone else who has temporarily lost hope and believed that the world is too far gone to be turned around, and to anyone who is struggling at home or at work, it is time to mobilize our collective pain to change everything.

And, just maybe, we will save the world in the process.

There is a lot of work to do, my friend, so let's get to it.

Together.

PART ONE

WHY WE MUST GO TOGETHER

CHAPTER 1

We Can Always Do Better:
The Death of Civility

*Civility is not something that automatically happens. Civil
societies come about because people want them to.*

—*Jimmy Bise Jr.*

Why are you going into that store, nigger?"

No, I am not recounting a near-daily occurrence for my mother as she grew up in deeply segregated Mississippi in the 1950s. I am drawing on my own personal—and relatively recent—experience of coming face-to-face with overt racism.

Four years ago on the Fourth of July, I drove into the parking lot of a local West Los Angeles grocery store at around 6 a.m. to pick up my favorite food on earth (crisp white peaches, in case you were wondering) before I went to the gym for an early-morning workout.

I chose to stop at a very upscale grocery store on the way to my gym for two reasons. One, the parking lot was relatively empty, so there wouldn't be much of a line. Two, that store is known for having large, firm peaches, rather than the nasty, mushy kind that are practically inedible. My goal was simple: Quickly grab a half-dozen yummy peaches, put in a solid workout at the gym, and then enjoy a relaxing day with my family barbecuing and completely unplugging from work and the other drama that was competing for attention in my mind.

Unfortunately, the universe had different plans for me on our nation's birthday.

As I left my parked car and walked through the nearly empty parking lot toward the grocery store's entrance, I noticed a very well-dressed blonde woman in her mid- to upper forties parked right next to the store's entrance, in a late-model BMW.

For some reason, her eyes were completely locked in on me as I walked closer to the entrance to the store. Do you know that creepy feeling when you *know* that someone is staring at you? I felt it, so to break the awkwardness in my mind, I made eye contact with her and smiled.

That's when she rolled down her car window, and with a hatefulness that I am ill-equipped to accurately convey on the page, she said the following to me:

"Why are you going into that store, nigger? You know that you can't afford

anything inside of there. You need to go back to Africa and let us celebrate this country in peace, you filthy monkey. You niggers make me sick."

Then she spit at me (and missed), and drove off.

The Post-Fireworks Hangover

I stood alone in stunned silence in the grocery store parking lot as I watched her car finally disappear from view. I remember helplessly looking around for someone to come to my aid after being the victim of a drive-by verbal assault. Unfortunately, no one was there to witness it.

In my forty-three years on this earth, I am certainly no stranger to racism, but admittedly (and thankfully), I have never experienced anything that was quite as in-my-face as that brief, fifteen-second encounter was.

I left the store without my white peaches, without completing my workout, and with far less faith in humanity than I had before I woke up that morning. My faith in humanity would continue to be tested as I shared my story with others throughout the day.

The responses varied.

Some friends narrowed their eyes as I told my story. *"Really, Shola? Come on, man, we live in West Los Angeles. That stuff doesn't happen here."* (Me: Well, it did).

Others immediately went the social justice route. *"Did you get her license plate number? You need to report her to the police and get her arrested!"* (Me: Yeah, because I'm sure that the commanders of the Los Angeles Police Department are going to deploy their overburdened resources to track down anonymous "name-callers" who hurl insults out of their car windows.)

Some felt that an eye-for-an-eye method would work best. *"Dude, I hope that you cursed her out for disrespecting you like that."* (Me: What would that prove?)

And, of course, there's always that one person you should never ask for advice. *"If that happened to me, I would have dragged that bitch out of her car and beat her ass in that parking lot."* (This one didn't even warrant a response.)

Admittedly, I felt defeated throughout the day as I thought about this situation. On the one hand, there was the rudeness and incivility that I faced, and on the other hand, there was the complete unwillingness of anyone to come up with a reasonable solution to fix it.

Enough was enough. We need solutions and we need them now.

Defining the Problem

Before we can discuss meaningful solutions—which is the purpose of this entire book—we must first gain crystal clarity about the problem we are currently up against.

The aforementioned parking lot encounter happened way back in 2014—a time that many people (myself included) now fondly look back on as the good ol' days. However, as we fast-forward to the time of this writing, interpersonal relations have taken a sharp nosedive.

This is not just my opinion, mind you. To support this contention, I chose to cite the research of experts in the field. Since 2010, global communications firms Weber Shandwick and Powell Tate, in partnership with KRC Research, have been studying how civility impacts Americans. Their yearly report, *Civility in America: The State of Civility*, offers one of the most comprehensive accounts of what is going on with regard to interpersonal relations in this country. Their definition of civility is simple and straightforward: *polite and respectful conduct and expression*. And their latest sobering and frightening report, *Civility in America VII*, illustrates how far we have fallen.

Ever since they have been conducting this research, the state of civility in America has never been worse than it is currently. And if you are paying attention, I am sure that you will concur with their findings. Specifically, their research found that Americans who believe that the United States has a major civility problem has reached a record high (69%).[1] Below are some additional troubling statistics supported by the research:

» 75% of Americans believe that incivility in America has reached crisis levels.

» 74% of Americans believe that we are losing stature as a civil nation.

» Americans encounter incivility nearly once a day (6.7 times in a seven-day week).

» 25% of Americans have experienced cyberbullying or incivility online (which may seem like an extremely low number, but it is up *three times* from 2011).

» Americans reported experiencing incivility almost everywhere—including on the road while driving, while shopping, at school, in their neighborhood, at social events, on public transportation, and even at places of worship.[2]

Also, regardless of your race, religious beliefs, financial situation, or even your health condition, no one seems to be safe from incivility in America. According to Weber Shandwick's thorough research, below are the groups who currently experience incivility most often:

» 77% black/African-American people

» 73% immigrants

» 72% women

» 72% lower-income people

» 71% homeless people

» 71% Muslims

» 70% LGBT people

» 69% Hispanics/Latinos

» 66% police officers

» 65% people with a physical disability

» 64% people with an intellectual disability

- » 64% refugees
- » 62% working-class people
- » 60% Native Americans
- » 58% white people
- » 58% Jewish people[3]

Digging deeper into the research, I found even more shocking data. Nearly two-thirds of Americans (63%) agree that people are currently more civil at work than outside of work.[4]

Wait . . . what?!

My jaw nearly hit the floor when I read this statistic for the very first time. As you might know, my entire professional career has been focused on addressing the widespread, damaging effects of workplace incivility. And, believe me, the current state of the working world is far from ideal. That is why I wrote an entire book to directly address this toxic issue, which is actively destroying productivity, careers, our health (mental, emotional, and physical), and lives all over the world as you are reading this. So, despite the current broken state of the workplace, for me to hear that nearly two-thirds of Americans feel safer from incivility *while at work than outside of work* is incredibly shocking, to say the least.

Okay, enough with the alarming statistics—please allow me to end with the least surprising statistic of all. It is also the main reason I believe that we are in this mess in the first place:

Ninety-four percent of Americans believe that they are always/ usually polite and respectful to others.[5]

Yes, even though incivility is currently more widespread than it has ever been in this country, the overwhelming majority of Americans are unwilling to take responsibility for any of it. To me, that final statistic— or, specifically, the underlying reason behind that statistic—is what we need to focus on in order to heal our world.

For this, we will need to refer to a brazen bank robbery, lemon juice, failed invisibility powers, and a crippling cognitive bias.

The Bank Robbery That Changed Everything

On April 19, 1995, a man named McArthur Wheeler did something so breathtakingly bizarre that it will likely be remembered in criminal history forever. In broad daylight, Wheeler attempted to rob not one, but *two* Pittsburgh banks, all while wearing no mask.

Confusing, right? Who in the world would attempt to rob a bank without wearing something to hide his face from the security cameras that are continuously filming every square inch of the place? McArthur Wheeler, that's who. So, why did he do it?

Because he smeared his entire face with lemon juice before committing the robberies.

I know, I know—now you are even more confused. Let me explain.

Wheeler realized that lemon juice is often used as invisible ink, so he made the highly questionable mental leap that if he covered his face with it, he would be made invisible to security cameras and he would be able to rob a bank with relative ease. Seriously, you cannot make up something like this.

To his credit, prior to the robberies, he did attempt to test his wonky theory by rubbing lemon juice all over his face and then taking a selfie with a Polaroid camera. Once the film eventually developed minutes later, his face was nowhere to be found on the image—it worked!

Actually, it didn't work at all. Most likely his camera wasn't working or he was pointing the camera in the wrong direction as he snapped the picture (if you are old enough to remember, trying to take a selfie with a traditional camera was not an easy task and the lemon juice probably didn't help). So he falsely believed that his strategy was rock-solid. Reportedly, his confidence in his strategy emboldened him to the point where he even smiled at security cameras on his way out of the banks!

Predictably, thanks to the abundance of clear security footage of his face, Wheeler was captured by the police hours later. Incredulous at the failure of his master plan, when he was arrested, he uttered the words that have nearly become iconic, "But I wore the juice!"

Before you dismiss him as someone who was high on drugs or intoxicated by cheap liquor (he was neither), or you choose to enjoy a hearty chuckle at his expense, what you and I should be doing instead is examining how much we may have in common with this guy.

The Dunning-Kruger Effect Is Born

The stunning incompetence of this failed robbery attempt grabbed the attention of many Americans, who were in complete disbelief that someone would think that this plan would work. It even ended up in the 1996 *World Almanac* the following year. But two men, in particular, were driven to look deeper into this to gain insight into the inner workings of many of our minds.

After reading about McArthur Wheeler's lemon-juice fiasco, David Dunning, a psychology professor at Cornell University, and one of his graduate students, Justin Kruger, decided to conduct a series of experiments. During their research, they found that people who scored the lowest on various assessments often rated their skill the highest. Yikes. Maybe this was more widespread than an individual trying to rob a couple of banks with a citrus-juice disguise. In general, are people like Wheeler—that is, clearly incompetent—too incompetent to realize their own incompetence? And, even more frighteningly, is this more common than we might have thought?

Dunning and Kruger believed so. In their well-known research paper, "Unskilled and Unaware of It: How Difficulties Recognizing One's Own Incompetence Lead to Inflated Self-Assessments," they argued the following:

When people are incompetent in the strategies they adopt to achieve success and satisfaction, they suffer a dual burden: Not only do they reach erroneous conclusions and make unfortunate choices, but their incompetence robs them of the ability to realize it. Instead, like Mr. Wheeler, they are left with the mistaken impression that they are doing just fine.[6]

Yes, you read that correctly. McArthur Wheeler felt that he was doing just fine as he boldly strode into those Pittsburgh banks with nothing but lemon juice to hide his face. This cognitive bias is now known as the Dunning-Kruger Effect, and it encompasses two fascinating ideas:

1. The least competent people are not only very poor self-assessors, but they often overestimate their competence, due largely to their ignorance about what it takes to be competent.

2. The same skills and knowledge that are needed to become truly competent at a task are often the *exact same skills* needed to realize that you are not competent at a task.

If you think about it, this makes complete sense. A perfect example of the Dunning-Kruger Effect was on the once-ubiquitous television show *American Idol*. Do you remember during the audition rounds when countless singers from all over the country would stand in front of the show's judges and belt out the most off-key, glass-shattering, auditory assaults imaginable on our unsuspecting eardrums? Even worse, do you remember when the judges politely (okay, maybe not so politely) told them after their ill-fated auditions that they were not good enough to advance to the next round of the competition?

They lost their minds. Some of the singers breathlessly attempted to convince the judges that they were the next big thing in pop music. Some stood in silent disbelief of the judges' failure to recognize their talent. Some even screamed and cursed angrily at the judges. And when the show's host, Ryan Seacrest, put a microphone in their faces afterward, almost all of them freely shared a misguided assessment that they were a multiplatinum pop star in the making. In their view, the problem was not their voices; it was that the judges were too stupid to see their talents.

That is the power of this crippling cognitive bias. Even though everyone who watched the show on television could clearly see—and hear—their incompetence, the incompetent ones not only could not see it, but they thought that they were the next Adele or Marvin Gaye. And before you think that this is limited to tone-deaf reality show contestants, this cognitive bias affects pretty much everyone, including medical school students, parents, newly licensed drivers, high-ranking politicians, your buddy who thinks he is hilariously funny (even though he's not), your colleagues, and, yes, even you and me.

I believe that this bias also plays a key role in why most of us believe that we are making this world a kinder place when we really are not. Only with this sobering realization can we take the first and, arguably, the most important step in breathing life back into civility in the world.

Yes, We Are the Raindrop

I once had a mentor who would often tell me that "there has never been a drop of rain that believed it was responsible for the flood." I believe that this is truer now more than ever. Whether we like it or not, *We are the raindrop responsible for the flood.*

Revisiting the research from Weber Shandwick, the fact that 94 percent of Americans *believe* that they are usually/always polite and respectful should cause us to take pause. Obviously, if 94 percent of Americans *actually were* always polite, then we wouldn't be mired in this civility crisis right now and there would be no reason for me to write this book. But let's face facts—that's not the reality we are currently confronting, is it?

It's even scarier to think that the overwhelming majority of people believe that they are not contributing to the current state of incivility in any way. I have counseled some of the most toxic bullying bosses who sincerely believed that they were kind people who cared deeply about the employees they supervised. One of them once told me, with a straight face, "How is my staff going to know that I care about them if I'm not constantly screaming at them?" Based on my conversations with him, there is no doubt in my mind that he would place himself in the 94 percent of usually/always polite people in the world. Heck, I'm willing to bet that if I could track down the woman who spit at me from her car window, she would likely place herself in that category, too. As crazy as this may sound, I doubt that she would view herself as being impolite. Chances are that she is able to sleep well at night because she believes that she spit at me because encouraging people like me to leave the country was what was best for her, her loved ones, and for America.

Not only do we have a civility crisis, but I will take it a step further—*we also have a self-awareness crisis.* Self-awareness is the conscious knowledge of your good and bad traits or, worded differently, it is about being honest and aware of the person you really are. And if you are being honest with yourself, you already know how tough it is to master the self-awareness game. Maybe you have a passive-aggressive side, perhaps you have bouts of moodiness, maybe you make excuses and don't take ownership, maybe there are times when you are the jerk in the room, or maybe other people don't enjoy being around you. The question that matters right now is this: *Do you know these things about yourself?*

If those things are true, then, yes, you are likely contributing to the plague of incivility in the world right now. You are not alone, I am a contributor, too—this is why we are the raindrop. It serves no one, especially ourselves, to think that we are absolved of any responsibility here.

So, as our first assignment in healing the world, I humbly ask that we adopt a simple mantra whenever we think about the civility crisis that we are facing: *I can always do better.*

No, it is not your boss and coworkers who can do better, the Republicans or the Democrats who can do better, your obnoxious neighbors who can do better, your significant other who can do better, the guy who cut you off on the freeway who can do better, your parents who can do better, or the Division of Motor Vehicles representative who hates her job who can do better. All of that may be true, of course— but that no longer matters. Creating a world where we go together requires the self-awareness that you and I can be kinder, that you and I can be more respectful, that you and I can be more empathetic and compassionate, and that you and I can always do better in terms of our interpersonal interactions.

Sure, it is more comfortable to believe that we are firmly in the 94 percent who are usually/always polite to others, but it is more useful to believe that we are not quite there yet. This also means that we will have to give up the joy of blaming others for this mess. *We are the raindrop.* And being the raindrop means that we are more powerful than we realize. Giving our power away by constantly assigning blame to others only reaffirms that we are helpless bystanders. We can take steps to fix this now, regardless of how others are acting. Viewing the world through this lens will provide us with the necessary edge to keep working on ourselves, to leave the world better than we found it, and ideally to create an example of civility so we can lead others.

I can do better, and I will. I need you to do better, too. But first, there is one thing left to do.

What Is the Source of Your Pain?

This entire book is about how much more we can do together than we can do alone. I also believe that a great many of our incivility problems stem from the fact that you and I have to do some important work on ourselves first.

The journey to go together will require us to be uncomfortable quite often, and the first stop on this road is to go within ourselves. And if we do this in earnest, we might not like what we find during this process. I am asking you to take a deep look into your fears, your biases, your insecurities, your behavior, and, most of all, your pain.

Unaddressed pain will not dissipate on its own. Ignoring our pain, denying its presence, or trying to cover it up with a myriad of vices will not weaken it, either. Despite our best efforts, our pain has a sneaky way of seeping out of us despite our best efforts to keep it hidden from others. It could range from consistently snapping at your loved ones after a long day at work to choosing to march in a hate rally while shouting divisive rhetoric from the top of your lungs. The source of these behaviors is often rooted in unexamined and unaddressed pain.

Do you know what the source of your pain is? If not, this is where we must begin. We must name our pain, understand our pain, and then sit with it. As you will find out, not only is the experience of pain uncomfortable, but so is the discovery of the source of it.

Whenever I see egregiously bad behavior, like the woman in the grocery store parking lot, I often think of how much pain she must be in. People who are hurting are the ones who hurt people the most. And when we're in a weakened state because of how much we're hurting, we can't effectively heal our world. We cannot show up and go together as broken individuals.

This requires a focused and steadfast commitment to self-discovery. If you are willing to do this work, you can begin the journey by answering these two questions:

1. In what ways do you believe that you can do better—specifically, with regard to the kindness and civility that you extend to others?

2. When you are not kind and civil toward others, what do you think is the underlying reason? Do your unkind and uncivil actions reflect unconscious or unexamined biases toward others? Unaddressed pain? Low self-esteem? Something else?

Taking the time to honestly answer those two questions (and, ideally, writing down your answers), and reviewing those answers daily will prepare you for the road ahead. Yes, incivility in America is as bad as it has ever been, but the key to reversing that trend lies with you and me becoming fully awakened to the source of our pain, and to the reality that we can—and we must—do better.

It is time to be introduced to the word that will help us to do just that.

CHAPTER 2

One Word That Will Change Everything: The Invincibility of Ubuntu

Everything that you are against weakens you.
Everything you are for empowers you.

—Dr. Wayne Dyer

U buntu.

Yes, I believe that philosophy behind this one word can change the world. I remember hearing the story where I was introduced to this transformative word for the first time.

As the story goes, years ago, there was an anthropologist who spent a significant amount of time with a tribe in an unspecified area of Africa. He was there to study the customs of this particular tribe, and on the day when he was about to leave to go back to his home country, he wanted to have some fun with the kids with whom he had spent so much time.

Earlier, the anthropologist had bought a lot of candy and other treats in the nearby city and, as a gesture of kindness, he placed all the goodies in a large basket tied with a ribbon. He then placed the basket under a tree, and he called the children of the tribe together to play a game.

The kids of the tribe stood a few yards away, and then he drew a line in the dirt with a stick. He told the children that in a moment he would yell "Now!" and at that moment, the children could race past the line in the dirt and grab as much candy as they could carry. The anthropologist predicted that it would be a complete free-for-all. If you have ever been to a children's birthday party when a piñata finally bursts open from repeated strikes with a stick, you know exactly what I am talking about.

That did not happen in this case.

As instructed, the kids stood together behind the line, and the anthropologist yelled "Now!" Then something magical happened.

One of the children yelled in response, "Ubuntu!" And the kids, almost instinctively, interlocked hands and joyfully ran to the baskets of goodies, *together.*

Dumbfounded, the anthropologist asked the kids what had just happened. They responded with a wisdom that is profound in its simplicity.

"How could any one of us be happy if all the others were sad?"

This is the essence of Ubuntu, and I believe that we can use this word to transform how we live, work, and lead in this world, starting today.

The Power of Ubuntu

The word Ubuntu (pronounced oo-BOON-too) means, "I am, because we are." It specifically refers to the power of our shared humanity, a deep level of kindness, consistent generosity, and our innate duty to support each other on this journey we call life. It is difficult to put the concept of Ubuntu into terms that the Western world can understand, but I believe that Archbishop Desmond Tutu did it best:

> Ubuntu [is] the essence of being human. Ubuntu speaks particularly about the fact that you can't exist as a human being in isolation. It speaks about interconnectedness. You can't be human all by yourself, and when you have this quality—Ubuntu—you are known for your generosity. We think of ourselves far too frequently as just individuals, separated from one another, whereas you are connected and what you do affects the whole world.[1]

Yes, Ubuntu is the essence of being human, and I am going to take it a step further. I believe that our humanity is severely diminished when we fail to incorporate the power of Ubuntu into our daily lives. As Archbishop Tutu brilliantly stated, none of us can exist as a human being in isolation—at least, not effectively. This inextricable connection to others has inspired people to do more than simply share candy with friends; it has saved lives, too.

In his compelling TED talk, titled "What I Learned from Nelson Mandela," wildlife activist Boyd Varty shared a harrowing story that involved his mentor and friend, Solly Mhlongo. On a particularly hot day in southern Africa, Boyd decided to wade into a river to cool off.

Unbeknownst to him, a crocodile was lurking in the shadows under a nearby tree. The crocodile immediately attacked him, repeatedly biting his right leg. As the crocodile attempted to rip off Boyd's leg, drag him underwater, or both, he was somehow able to kick himself free. His friend Solly, who was on the riverbank nearby, saw that Boyd's leg was broken and mangled beyond recognition, and that he was still in grave danger.

With a bloodthirsty crocodile literally in between him and Boyd, without hesitation, Solly waded into waist-high water, threw his badly injured friend over his shoulder, walked him back to safety on the riverbank, and took him to get medical attention.

As Boyd describes it, it was as "natural as breathing" for Solly to walk into a situation where his potential death was a definite possibility. It made no sense for him to behave in any other way. Boyd's pain was Solly's pain because to him, they are connected by a bond—not just as friends, but as human beings. That is the power of Ubuntu. We are social beings whose natural state is to care for others. When you do not see yourself as separate from anyone else on this planet, you are willing to do some pretty amazing things.

Before you dismiss Solly's courageous act as a random feat of superheroism on some faraway continent, I would advise you to look more deeply at this behavior. Think of the most catastrophic events in recent American history. Mass shootings with dozens of innocent people killed. Hurricanes, floods, and other natural disasters that have left entire communities in ruin. September 11, 2001.

Have you ever noticed how people react during those tragedies or immediately afterward? Two things happen, invariably.

The first is that when another person is bleeding from a gunshot wound, about to drown in a flood, trapped under a pile of rubble, or in any other type of mortal danger, it is our natural instinct to rush in and help him—often with complete disregard for our own safety and well-being. Three years ago, while I was driving home one evening, I witnessed a woman who was accidentally hit by a car while she was riding her bicycle. She flew off her bike and landed awkwardly and violently on the side of the road, with moderate injuries. The next thing that I remember, at least a dozen other strangers and I abandoned our cars in the middle of a busy Los Angeles street (many of us with our keys still in the ignition!), and rushed across the busy street to lend aid or comfort to her. I think of that moment often. I did not even think or consciously decide to help her. One moment I was in my car driving home, and the next I was at a complete stranger's side in hopes of offering comfort to her.

Here is the second thing I have noticed. When the stakes are the highest—say, in a tragedy like a mass shooting, a raging wildfire that is putting homes in danger, or a dangerous flood—also invariably, the divisions that we clung to *before those tragedies* instantly disappear *during those tragedies*. In those pivotal life-and-death moments, I have never seen anyone stop to ask, before they lent a helping hand, "Hey, are you a Republican or Democrat?" Or "I'm curious, what country were your parents born in?" Or "Do you believe in same-sex marriage?" Or "Have you chosen Jesus Christ as your lord and savior?"

No. What they do, whether they realize it or not, is connect with our shared humanity, instead of focusing on our differences. *That* is Ubuntu.

Before you think that I am calling on you to wrestle crocodiles to show the world how much you love humanity, let me be clear about one thing. This is about shifting our focus from being inwardly focused (or focused only on our inner circle), and expanding it so we act in a manner that will be for the betterment of humanity. Why must we wait for the specter of death to threaten us or others to tap into this natural state of connection? If we decided to do this now, today, we would be more generous, more thoughtful, more loving, and more willing to take action to help others, because doing so helps us as well.

In the Introduction of this book, Jordan and I wondered what it would mean for the world if our collective mind-set were refocused on the powerful concept of Ubuntu. I want you to imagine this, too. Can you imagine a world where we acted as if we were connected to our colleagues, our neighbors, and everyone else we encounter in our day-to-day travels? How would it change the degree of kindness and respect that you showed to others—especially to people you previously believed were different from you?

Everything from refilling the empty coffeepot in the breakroom at the office to jumping into crocodile-infested waters to save a friend are examples of Ubuntu. That is the essence of "I am, because we are."

Sadly, though, if you turn on the news, look around at your workplace, or take a walk around your neighborhood, chances are that you will notice that many people in America do not think or behave in that manner.

I think I know why.

The Solution to Separateness

We cannot heal this world by operating as if we are separate from others. If anything, I believe that viewing the world in this way only serves to widen the divide that we are experiencing now.

If you think about it, the ones who are hurting the world the most are the ones who are the most steadfastly self-focused and single-mindedly concerned about what is in it for them before they take action. They are the ones who believe in isolation and separateness over the collective strength of our shared humanity. I can promise you that you will not find any examples in the entirety of human history where this mind-set has improved the world in a meaningful way.

Why? Because separation makes it much easier to dehumanize others, which is the antithesis of Ubuntu. If you are unable to see yourself as connected to others or, worse, you are unable to see certain people or groups as human beings, it opens the door wide for all sorts of atrocities to be perpetrated.

What causes people to bully others mercilessly at work, shrug with ambivalence when a stranger in another state loses her home and her family in a hurricane, rape someone in a college dorm room, murder someone for a new pair of basketball shoes, open fire on a school full of children, or go to war as a nation and intentionally kill hundreds of thousands of people (many of whom did not ask to participate in the war)? My answer is a failure to see and respect our shared humanity. If we view other humans simply as a means to satisfy our self-involved ends, instead of as sentient beings with feelings, emotions, hopes, and fears, we don't worry about hurting them or seeing them in pain. If we allow this approach to become the norm, we will devolve to a point where seeing and accepting human suffering become as routine to us as swiping on our smartphone screen. This is not okay, and all of us are worse off because of it.

So, how do we stop hurting others, stop ignoring the pain of others, acknowledge our shared humanity, and live the spirit of Ubuntu?

The key is empathy.

Empathy is the ability to understand another person's perspective, or the ability to feel what another person feels, and that can change everything. In the example of the African kids who held hands as they ran together to gather the candy, or the story of Solly saving his friend Boyd's life, both the African children and Solly were fueled by empathy. It could be argued that Ubuntu is not only empathy in action, but the height of emotional intelligence.

If we could feel the pain of others, would we be willing to hurt them? The answer, unequivocally, is no, because hurting others would be no different than hurting yourself. This is the brilliance of the Ubuntu philosophy—our joy, our failures, our successes, and our pain are shared. *Literally.* There is a built-in benefit to caring for others because, besides making the world a more pleasant place to live, it also directly benefits us. This is why one of the most meaningful exercises that we can engage in to heal our world is to strengthen our connection to others through empathy.

Developing Empathy through Curiosity

The very good news is that empathy is not an "Either you have it or you don't" kind of a deal. With the exception of a severe head injury or health-related cognitive issues, empathy can be taught and cultivated in just about anyone.

Like most things, though, developing empathy is about the willingness to put in the work. Putting in the work is not a given, considering that many people would rather stay entrenched in their own self-righteousness than take a tiny step to understand another person's perspective.

So how do you connect with someone if you don't feel connected to him or her?

Become curious.

Sure, you can say that what fuels the people with whom you vehemently disagree does not pique your curiosity, but I would argue that the lack of curiosity about those views is exactly what got us into this mess in the first place. The unwillingness to learn about another person's fears and pain—or, worse, to attack them because of it—will only widen the divide. As Archbishop Tutu once said, "If you want peace, you don't talk to your friends. You talk to your enemies."

Obviously, this is not easy. Last year, I watched a well-attended white supremacist rally on the news and, admittedly, as I looked into the eyes of the participants, connection, empathy, and Ubuntu were not on the short list of thoughts running through my mind at the time. I was scared. I was angry. Most of all, I wanted to protect my own humanity by separating myself from these types of people who had clearly lost theirs.

Then I challenged myself to do something that I often discuss at my workplace seminars: **Remain curious and reserve judgment.**

Judgment is one of the quickest and most effective ways to shut down connection with others. And, if we are being honest, most judgments that we make about others are based on incomplete information. Curiosity, on the other hand, keeps us open to the possibility that there is something about the situation that we don't fully understand. The unfortunate reality is that *we all* think that we are the good guys, and I doubt that any of those marchers believed that they were engaging in behavior that was evil—even though their actions hurt and scared a great many people.

And, yes, initially, I judged those hate rally marchers quite viciously. But something happened when I shifted to curiosity by asking myself, "I wonder what is going on with those people that I don't know about?"

Digging deeper into my curiosity, I could view these people differently. They were broken, powerless, and, most of all, very, very scared.

Before I go further, let me address what you might be thinking.

"Okay, Shola, so are you saying that we need to look at these degenerate racists *and empathize with them?* What's next, empathizing with child abusers, murderers, rapists, and other deviants? Isn't this one tiny step away from making excuses for the inexcusable?"

Not at all. **Nothing is acceptable about hurting another person.** There are lines that should never be crossed, and hurting people is one of them. (I will address this more in the next chapter.)

In my forty-three years of life—half of which is in the people profession—I have seen men and women victimized in ways that defy description, and the last thing I am interested in doing is empathizing with the perpetrators. There will always be extreme examples where empathy is not the answer, and it would be foolish not to acknowledge this.

However, that said, in the overwhelming majority of everyday cases, where you are choosing to separate yourself from others because of your differing viewpoints, I believe that empathy can serve as a bridge to connection.

Equally as important, my hope is that by tuning in to our curiosity, we can use that curiosity to better understand what is behind our nation's trend toward incivility, and ideally use this knowledge to bring about a more civil society. If we truly want hateful behavior to stop, then we are going to have to do a whole lot more than engaging in name-calling and judgments. By dehumanizing people, not only are we dehumanizing ourselves (I am, because we are—remember?), but we are doing nothing to solve the problem, either. Instead, we need as many people as possible onboard with the goal of trying to understand why people do these uncivil things in the first place.

In certain situations, empathizing with someone will be difficult, if not impossible, and, in those cases, at the very least, stay curious. It is from this awakened state that we can find solutions to these seemingly insurmountable problems.

So, do you have the courage and mental fortitude to stay curious about people you really do not like or respect?

Let's find out.

Practicing Ubuntu

Let's make all this practical. I want you to think of someone you have a fundamental disagreement with—perhaps a colleague, a friend, or a family member who has the polar opposite political views that you have. Got that person in mind? Good. To make this easier, let's call this person "Uncle George." Here are two things you can do to increase connection with Uncle George, while still staying true to your values.

1. Practice being on the other side.

This can be done without Uncle George being present, and it is a very challenging exercise. Instead of simply having an open mind, can you actively advocate the virtues of Uncle George's viewpoints?

For example, pretend that you would be given $10,000 in cold, hard cash if you could convincingly argue Uncle George's political views against someone who shares your political ideology. Could you win? Do you have what it takes to sincerely find virtues in the political candidates Uncle George voted for?

I fully understand if the mere thought of this exercise is causing you to become slightly nauseous—I felt the same way initially. Who wants to try to understand why someone has beliefs that are the exact opposite of yours? Not many people—and, in many ways, that is exactly the problem.

Maintaining separateness and picking sides (or, in some cases, trying to destroy the other side) may sound more appealing, but as the internationally known author and television personality Dr. Phil McGraw would say, "How's that working for you?" From my vantage point, it is not working at all. If you don't believe me, revisit the civility statistics cited in the previous chapter. For different results, we must take different actions, and this exercise is very effective in helping people to broaden their viewpoints and to see the world in a more inclusive manner. Think of this as your own personal empathy workout. And, like other workouts that could positively affect your overall well-being, it is one that most people would rather make excuses not to do.

If we want to heal the world and create a spirit of Ubuntu, we don't have that luxury.

2. Actively listen (for real).

The next time the topic of politics happens to come up with Uncle George, instead of trying to school him about how he is on the wrong side of history or, worse, trying to change his mind (which, as we both know, will never happen), try to understand him instead.

Humans like to feel understood, and the willingness to understand someone's point of view can go a long way toward building mutual respect, civility, and connection. Here are a few ways to do this well:

> » As noted earlier, withhold judgment and listen with sincere interest to learn more about his viewpoint.

- » Paraphrase his points to make sure you're understanding his perspective. You could begin by stating, "Keep me honest. It sounds like you're saying . . ."
- » Stay respectful. When you disagree with him (and you will), instead of rolling your eyes, loudly sighing, or interrupting him, practice slowing down (or even staying silent) to remain calm when you are feeling frustrated.
- » Ask questions or dig deeper by saying, "Tell me more . . ."
- » Reject your need to be right—there is no winner in this discussion. If anything, both of you should feel as if you won when you are done.

Please note that I did *not* say that you need to agree with Uncle George. This is solely about creating a deeper connection with someone you might not normally connect with. It will always be easier to have political and philosophical discussions with people who believe the exact same things that you do, but I would argue that that will not change the world.

It takes courage to understand someone who thinks differently from us (as mentioned earlier, more on this in the next chapter), and by listening actively, you might realize that the pain and fear that is driving Uncle George's actions are the exact same ones that are also driving yours, too.

What Really Matters Is Connection

Ubuntu is about human connection, and not only can it save the world, it might even save your life.

Harvard University's world-famous, seventy-five-year-long Grant study (the longest study of human development in existence), followed hundreds of men for nearly a century. Harvard psychiatrist Robert Waldinger, who took over the study in 2003, shared one of the key takeaways from it in a 2015 TED talk, titled "What Makes a Good Life? Lessons from the Longest Study on Happiness":

The first is that social connections are really good for us, and that loneliness kills. It turns out that people who are more socially connected to family, to friends, to community, are happier, they're physically healthier, and live longer than people who are less well connected.[2]

It would be foolish, if not dangerous, to ignore the reality that science supports this, our history supports this, and, dare I say, what we feel in the deepest part of our soul supports this: *Our health and happiness depend on our willingness to connect with others.* If you are still not a believer, you could wait until you are broken and alone on your deathbed to make this realization with near-mathematical certainty, but that is hardly advisable.

The choices that all of us make from this point on will cement our legacy. And as you look into the eyes of your children, grandchildren, or others you will leave behind once you die, you will be held accountable for these choices as they carry on in your absence. So ask yourself:

» Did you choose to stay asleep by playing favorites, picking sides, and building walls, or did you awaken to the reality that we are all in this together?

» Did you choose to dehumanize those who are different, or did you choose to acknowledge our shared humanity?

» Did you choose to fight to stay separated and isolated, or did you choose to connect meaningfully with others?

» Did you choose to walk alone, or did you choose to go together?

And no, you cannot opt out of making a choice: Your legacy is a mandatory final assignment that is due on the day you die. And when you submit your completed work with your final breath, the world will be counting on you to make the right choices. There is too much at stake not to be fully conscious about the stakes here.

In the spirit of transparency, the path to making Ubuntu our reality only gets harder from here. If you are ready, I will walk with you every step of the way on our journey.

We're in this together, my friend. *I am, because we are.*

Ubuntu.

CHAPTER 3

It Is Always Safer to Stand Up: The Uncomfortable Truth about Saving the World

The hottest places in hell are reserved for those who, in times of great moral crisis, maintain their neutrality.

—Dante Alighieri

So far, we have covered the civility problem that we are up against in Chapter 1, and the philosophy of Ubuntu and how we can use it to address this issue in Chapter 2. Now, in this chapter, it is time to discuss having the courage to do something with this information.

It may be easy to imagine the author of a book like this as someone who has it all figured out, or someone who has very little fear when it comes to taking action. I can assure you that neither is the case with me. I am no guru by any stretch of the imagination—I am a regular guy steeped in insecurities and fears who is simply passionate about making the world a kinder place.

I am assuming that you feel the same way, too. And if you choose to walk on this path with me, thankfully you do not have to be fearless, free from self-doubt, or have all the answers. What you will need is the one trait that neither of us can do without: **Courage.**

It takes courage to stand up for what you believe in. It takes courage to confront bad behavior. It takes courage to reach out to a group of people you have never spoken to before. It takes courage to admit that your actions have contributed to this problem and that you were wrong.

Chances are that you already know all that. What you might not know is that it is far safer to exhibit courage by jumping into the game and taking action than it will ever be to sit on the sidelines and do nothing.

I will never forget when I made that life-altering realization.

The Reward for Abuse

Nine years ago in November, I visited a large electronics store in Los Angeles in hopes of using a $50 gift card that I had received for my birthday toward the purchase of a digital camera that I had been drooling over for months. My wife Amber and I were expecting our first baby the following month, and I wanted to make sure that I had a high-quality camera to record our new family memories.

With my gift card in my hand, I remember parking next to a very old, beat-up, red Toyota sedan with a transparent trash bag serving as its passenger-side window. I tend to get lost in parking lots easily, so I try to remember every possible detail about where I park so that I could find my car afterward—and that car was very easy to remember.

Once inside the store, and after a fairly easy search, I discovered that my camera was in stock and in the color I was looking for, too. And if that was not enough good news, as an added bonus, the price was $40 less than advertised. Perfect! Everything was going exactly according to my plan.

Well, not exactly.

Although I was feeling pretty good about my luck up until this point, what happened next has stayed with me for almost a decade.

As I walked up to the cash register ready to pay for my new gadget, I could not help but notice a tall, thin, blonde-haired woman in a pinstriped business suit who looked incensed about something. The reason I could not help but notice her is that she practically knocked me over so that she could get into the checkout line before I did.

"No big deal," I silently reasoned to myself. "This lady doesn't even have anything in her cart. She'll probably be done in a minute or so, and then I can go home and play with my new camera."

I could not have possibly been more wrong.

The woman in the pinstriped suit locked eyes with the helpless, college-aged young man who was working at that particular cash register. Without warning, she struck like a black mamba attacking a hamster. This unfortunate guy had no chance. After the cashier politely asked how he could be of service to her, she slammed her fist on the counter and began her tirade.

"Hey asshole! (Side note #1: Yes, that is how she started the interaction.) You're telling me that you don't have any more Xboxes in this store? I can't believe this bullshit! Do you realize that I drove all the way from Brentwood to get here?! (Side note #2: Brentwood is not very far from this store.) My son's birthday is tomorrow, and I'll be damned if I don't leave this store with an Xbox. You know what, you fat piece of garbage? Just get out of my sight and get your manager before you have a real problem on your hands. Why are you still standing here, doughboy? Are you retarded?! I said, GO!"

Wow.

The entire front of the store came to a standstill during this woman's bizarre tirade. And with the eyes of many customers and colleagues locked in on the situation like a car wreck on the freeway, the cashier helplessly stood frozen with tears welling up in his eyes. Visibly and understandably shaken, he slowly lowered his head and shuffled pitifully to the customer service desk where he feebly motioned for his manager to assist him, before he disappeared out of sight.

Meanwhile, the angry lady kept ranting to anyone who was within earshot that there was *no way in hell* that her son was going to miss out on anything, especially on his birthday. Unfortunately for her son, it looks like he already missed out on having a mother to teach him the finer points of civility and kindness, too, but that's another story.

This story does not have a happy ending. After her abusive tirade, the manager informed the angry woman that his store was currently out of stock of Xboxes, but he called a nearby store that was less than five miles away, and that store would be holding one for her. And for her trouble, he gave her a $50 gift card in hopes of "making things right."

Wait . . . what?!

I could not believe my eyes. Did this store manager just *reward a customer* for viciously abusing one of his staff members? At that point, I was so disgusted that I left my prized digital camera on the counter, gave my $50 gift card to the guy behind me in line, and sadly walked back to my car. To this day, I have not set foot back in that store. It was what happened next that has haunted me for the past nine years.

As I got into my car, I noticed through the makeshift, plastic trash-bag window of the red Toyota parked next to me, that there was now a person sitting inside. I glanced over as I put my key into the ignition, only to see that it was the cashier who was the target of the screaming woman's attack just a few minutes earlier. He was slumped down over the steering wheel and was sobbing so loudly that I could hear him from inside my car with the doors and windows closed. To say that my heart broke for this kid would be a huge understatement. Enough was enough. I needed to take action.

At that moment, something clicked in my brain, and it has stayed in the on position ever since then. I had to do something to address this problem and stop it from ever happening again.

And contrary to what you might be thinking, the problem that needed to be fixed was not the abusive customer or the spineless manager.

The problem was me.

The Shame of Staying on the Sidelines

As I reflect on that moment nine years ago in that store, the one thing that stays with me the most was that *I said nothing and did nothing.*

In a moment where I could have offered some meaningful assistance to that young man, I sat on the sidelines like a coward. As I watched that customer verbally eviscerate the cashier, I could have intervened. I was literally the closest person to that woman as she started screaming at the cashier. Instead, I lowered my head and uncomfortably fiddled with my cell phone. I worked for years in retail, and I know that rewarding abusive customer behavior is the worst thing that you can do for staff morale (not to mention an unethical business practice). But as I passed by the manager on my way out of the store, I still did and said nothing. And then, a few short weeks later, while I was watching television, the following quote flashed across the screen and I knew that the Universe meant it for me. It is the same quote that I included at the beginning of this chapter: "The hottest places in hell are reserved for those who, in times of great moral crisis, maintain their neutrality."

What you might not know about me is that I despise confrontation. I abhor it. And up until that moment in the parking lot, avoiding conflict, keeping the peace, and remaining neutral were three of my most polished skills. Things have changed quite a bit since then.

Mind you, I still loathe confrontation (I mean, seriously—if you love confrontation and drama, isn't that a little weird?), but the difference now is that I will engage in confrontation when necessary, without hesitation. Nine years later, my buddies now call me SVU, short for Special Victims Unit, because I am always jumping in the middle of situations to help people.

Even though I did not know it at the time, as I sat in my car next to the cashier's on that late autumn evening, I experienced Ubuntu for the first time. His pain was now my pain, and I sincerely felt it as my own. Once you experience that sensation, it consumes you. As I pointed out earlier, confrontation is still extremely uncomfortable for me, but it pales in comparison to the searing discomfort of knowing that you could have alleviated someone else's pain, but you didn't heed the call.

Of course, it is certainly possible to feel some sense of security while sitting on the sidelines and remaining neutral. Here is what I know now, however: *Your safety is an illusion.* Whether you choose the immediate discomfort of engaging in necessary conflict, or the delayed discomfort of doing nothing, you will never be completely safe from risk, fear, or pain in any uncertain situation. Is it possible that if I had jumped to that young cashier's defense, that the woman could have unleashed the full fury of her rage on me instead of him? *Of course.* In fact, based on how unhinged she seemed, I think that would have been a likely outcome.

Here's the difference, though—and it is a big one: The pain and fear that I *might have* experienced by being her verbal punching bag while I defended the cashier would have been temporary. On the other hand, the shame that I have felt for the past nine years, brought on by allowing my fear to stop me from supporting someone who needed help, is permanent.

It is always safer to stand up for kindness, love, and in support of another human being who needs our help, than it will ever be to remain neutral. I can't speak about what drove Solly to wade into a crocodile-infested river to save his friend, as chronicled in the previous chapter, but I am assuming he also realized that being in the river was safer than remaining on shore. Think about that for a moment.

Admittedly, I still fantasize about how I would have handled the electronics store debacle differently if it happened today, but what's done is done. However, what is far from done is the work that you and I still need to do to heal this world, and ideally, re-create it in the spirit of Ubuntu.

There are two things that we must do, specifically—and courage is needed for both of them.

1. Standing up to bigotry, hate, and intolerance

As I type these words and look at the world around me, it is clear that we are not in a great place. In fact, I feel that in terms of intolerance, bigotry, and hatefulness, we are sliding backward as a society.

In response to this, I am going to ask you to stand up and not sit silently in the face of bigotry and hate. If you have anyone in your life who believes that it is acceptable to hate brown people, women, Jews, Muslims, foreigners, members of the LGBTQ community (or any other marginalized group), and you continue to break bread with these people without directly addressing it, then, unfortunately, you are part of the problem. Your silence serves no one.

If you choose to stand up, this is what it means for you.

It means that if your Aunt Suzanne finds it acceptable to sling racist slurs around the Thanksgiving dinner table, it is up to you to tell her that hate is not welcome in your home (the urgency of this is multiplied by a thousand if Aunt Suzanne is spouting off her vitriol in front of little children). It also means that if your fraternity buddies think that it is funny to tell rape jokes about women (or, worse, actually harass women), you will immediately tell them to knock it off, or do the responsible thing and make them stop. And, yes, it means that if a random person starts to publicly bully a person based on her race, religion, sexual orientation, or for any other reason, I am asking you to stand in support of the targeted person instead of looking the other way.

Sounds scary, doesn't it? I understand if you feel that way, but I need you to get over your fear, quickly. What really should scare you is a future where we excuse the inexcusable in the name of maintaining neutrality, chasing the ghost of safety, and avoiding conflict.

Please don't take the easy road on this. Don't say, "Well, that's just how Aunt Suzanne is. I know that she says some awful things, but deep down, she's really a great person . . ." *Is she, though?* I'm sure that the people who attended the hate rally cited in the previous chapter had folks back home offering the same sorry defense as they silently watched their loved ones terrorize innocent people.

Like bullies in the workplace, many of them are able to continue perpetrating their reign of terror simply because it is easier for the rest of us to remain quiet and do nothing. *Enough with the silence.* It is time to address these people. It is up to you to tell them to stop. And if they won't, then maybe it's time for you to sincerely question how—and why—they still have a coveted spot in your inner circle.

In the last chapter, I mentioned the importance of empathy and remaining curious, and that still holds true. To prevent future incivility, we must be curious to learn more about the cause of these mind-sets and refrain from judgment as we work toward solutions. However, in the moment that others are being *actively hurt* by incivility, hate, and intolerance, it is up to us to take action to make it stop—whether it is at the office holiday party, your sorority house, on social media, in a department store, or in the privacy of your own home.

I understand that it is scary to stand up. It would be far easier if someone else did it, but, as you already know, *there is no one else coming.* No one at the electronics store was willing to stand up for the cashier, and, believe me, there were a lot of people there who could have done something. And if you are being honest, no one at Thanksgiving dinner is probably willing to stand up to Aunt Suzanne's hateful comments, either. It would be easier for all parties involved to enjoy the turkey and the football game, avoid making a scene, and embrace the delusion that Aunt Suzanne will come to her senses one of these days.

The bad news is that the easy road does not work for difficult problems. Instead, it is far more useful to take the challenging road of standing up by directly and firmly saying, "Aunt Suzanne, please stop using that word in my house—I find it offensive." Standing up when we are scared—and accepting that doing so will be messy—is the uncomfortable truth about saving the world.

And, despite the discomfort, you can do it. If you want to see positive change before you die, you are being called to make it happen. The hero in this story is, and always has been, you.

2. Connecting to others who are different

When I was seventeen years old, I enrolled in a New England prep school to complete a postgraduate year. Oftentimes, when kids pursue a postgraduate year, it is because they want to play a sport in college, and they need an extra year to help their bodies mature and become fully prepared for the rigors of college athletics. Admittedly, I planned on playing college basketball after my postgraduate year, but that was far from my reason for being there. I had a dream of becoming a writer and a journalist, and this school had a phenomenal writing program.

I was excited to begin my new academic journey, and then it came crashing down within the first ten minutes of my first class at that school.

After struggling to pronounce my name, my teacher for that class looked me up and down, and said dismissively in front of the entire class, "I bet that you'd rather be dunking a basketball than sitting in this class, huh?"

Ugh. I felt the eyes of twenty complete (and mostly white) strangers staring at me, as I clumsily responded, "Actually, no. This is where I want to be."

For a teenager simply trying to fit in at a new school, that forty-five-second exchange was one of the most brutal interactions of my young life. On a positive note, it ended up being one of the most formative moments, too.

It inspired me to write an article about the incident that was published in the school newspaper. It was also the first time in my life that I had ever shared my writing publicly. The article was very well received, and it went as viral as an article could go in 1993. Afterward, the teacher apologized profusely. It was a learning experience for both of us.

Despite our unfortunate first encounter, I sincerely believe that the teacher is not a bad person. He had biases and was woefully misinformed about me. Most of all, he recognized those biases when I brought them to his attention. He saw a young, tall, slender black kid, with baggy clothes and, for whatever reason, his first thought was not that I would be a future author, or that I could explain trigonometric parallax with ease—which I could do at the time. Instead, he saw someone who was into dissecting zone defenses with pinpoint passes and reverse dunking basketballs (things I could also do at the time).

You and I are not unlike my former teacher. All of us carry stereotypes, biases, and misinformation about other people who are not like us. Usually, these are formed by television, movies, political pundits, our parents, or they come from our own limited personal experience. Left unexamined, they can widen the divide in our country instead of closing it.

This is where you—or, more specifically, your courage—come in. I believe that the unfortunate situation with my teacher, and others like it, could be greatly reduced if we simply took the time to connect with people who are different from us. The teacher admitted to me that his limited exposure to young black men led him to believe that the majority of them are primarily focused on athletics, because that was the case with the majority of the black students who had attended that school for a postgraduate year.

In addition to courage, this will also require very real effort. Specifically, this effort will require you to leave the safety of your comfort zone, which is something that most people do not like to do. In this regard, I am asking you not to be like most people. I want you to go to events, places of worship, restaurants, social organization meetings, and celebrations where you will meet people who are not like you. Hang out with people of different cultures, people of different religions, people of different sexual orientations, and learn about them. I believe that one of the most powerful ways to develop your courage, empathy, and connection to others is by having the experience of being a minority. Once you do, you will likely realize that you are more similar to others than you once believed.

Could you look silly if you say something dumb in a new and unfamiliar situation? Maybe, and that is completely okay—mistakes are easily forgiven if you are sincerely putting in an effort to connect. Just like anything that is new, you will not get it 100 percent right, initially. Perhaps people may be distrusting of your motives, and that is also fine—just stick with it, and do not let your fears and insecurities keep you from making connections with others. As mentioned earlier, the far easier alternative is to stay within the comfort of your own tribe, whose members consistently think, vote, and pray exactly the way you do. There is a huge risk in doing this, though. It would require you to forgo the meaningful change, growth, and human connection that can only happen outside the safety of your comfort zone.

Yes, I know that the idea that life happens outside our comfort zones may sound clichéd, but I find a great deal of value in this mindset. From my experience, the only things that I found inside of my comfort zone were stagnation, complacency, an intense boredom, and the road toward a slow death. On the other hand, the best of what life has to offer—namely, meaningful growth, varied experiences, overcoming the fear of the unknown, and possibly, healing our divided world—can only happen if we are willing to be temporarily uncomfortable in order to experience it.

This is what it means to lean into our discomfort. The reality is that we cannot run away from what is currently separating us if we want to go together. The road to healing requires much of us, and we must have clarity about what lies ahead. There may be difficult, but necessary, conversations with loved ones who harbor bigoted and hateful views. There may be people who will laugh at you, mock you, or completely misunderstand you for willingly choosing to connect with others who are different from you. You may have to examine your own beliefs that have unconsciously guided you toward separateness instead of togetherness.

At this point, you have a life-altering decision to make as you step toward the edge of your comfort zone—you can either lean into your discomfort, or you can run away from it. My hope is that you will stand up and lean in, because we cannot go together until you make this commitment.

This is just the preliminary work. We know that incivility and separateness are the key problems. We know that the philosophy of Ubuntu is the mind-set that can fix these issues, and that tapping into our courage is the only way we will find success on our journey together.

The world cannot be actively changed from the sidelines. To do this well, you have to be an active participant by choosing to stand up when it would be easier not to.

Thankfully, this is not about doing what is easy. It is about changing how we live, work, and lead, together.

Let's begin.

PART TWO

LIVE TOGETHER

CHAPTER 4

Fear or Love:
The Only Decision
That Matters

Love is what we are born with. Fear is what we learn.

—Marianne Williamson

Six years ago, a man named James left his job as a beloved senior director in the corporate sector to take on a new challenge. After eleven years in that role, and due in large part to his consistently high performance, he decided to take on a heightened level of responsibility as an executive for a troubled medical center on the East Coast.

What you need to know about James is that this man is the complete package in every sense of the word—wildly intelligent, a high performer, charismatic, hardworking, and relentlessly kind. Without question, James is the ideal person to be placed in a leadership position in any industry. From what I have recently heard, the folks he left behind in his previous job are still mourning his departure years after as you are reading these words.

It was not all sunshine, rainbows, and unicorns for him, though, in his new position.

James had been revered at his previous job for doing something that almost became his undoing at his new job. Wait for it, because it is pretty shocking. Are you ready?

He signed off on all his emails with "Love, James."

In his first week at his new job at the medical center, he sent out a short email to all the employees to introduce himself. And, as he has done in every email for the better part of a decade—but for the first time at his new job—he signed it as he usually does: "Love, James."

Those two words nearly shut down the entire hospital. Yes, you read that correctly. It was not an Ebola outbreak, a failed Joint Commission visit, or a nursing strike. Things almost came to a halt because of those two simple, well-meaning words.

Within minutes of the email being sent, James's peers in the executive suite called an emergency meeting to address this "disturbing issue." As the executives of the medical center huddled around the boardroom wringing their hands about how to deal with the "Love-Gate" scandal caused by the new guy, James walked past the boardroom and noticed that his new colleagues looked extremely stressed out, so he walked in and asked what was up.

And at that moment, they attacked.

James was lectured about professionalism, what it means to be a leader, and that signing emails with "Love" is not an accepted part of the medical center culture.

After quietly listening to the united stance against bringing love into the workplace, James asked a simple question to his executive peers that still remains unanswered to this day:

"Is it worse to end an email with 'love,' or to communicate in a manner that inspires distrust and fear?"

Crickets.

Their silence spoke volumes, but not wanting to make waves in his new job, after that day, James signed all his subsequent business communications "Sincerely, James." All the while, he watched his executive peers instill fear with harsh, impersonal, and cold communications.

James only lasted at that medical center for a little over a year, and while he was able to make some inroads into the company culture during that time, he left to lead another organization with love and positivity. In the meantime, that medical center where he formerly worked is floundering by endangering its patients due to poor team cohesion, ineffective communication, and abysmally low employee engagement.

When asked why he left, and why the medical center is continuing to fail, his answer was powerful and one that we should heed.

"They chose fear over love."

Choosing to Turn on the Light

Sure, we could use this space to debate the appropriateness of signing off on business emails with "Love," but I am interested in having a more meaningful discussion about an age-old question: Are you choosing fear or love?

Various spiritual teachers have boiled it down to the simplicity of those two life-altering options.

Unfortunately, that is also part of the problem. The simplicity behind the idea that our actions are often driven by only one of two sources will cause many people to dismiss this as a woo-woo, head-in-the-clouds, painfully simplistic, mentally soft delusion that does not address the complexities or the harsh realities of our current world.

Those people are dead wrong. There is nothing basic about choosing love over fear. Perhaps we need to look at this choice in a new way. World-renowned spiritual teacher and best-selling author Marianne Williamson once explained the difference between love and fear with a power metaphor.

> The relationship of love to fear is the same as the relationship of light to dark. Darkness is not a thing, *it's the absence of a thing*. So, if you want to get rid of darkness, you can't hit it with a baseball bat—you turn on the light, and the darkness disappears.[1]

No pun intended, but I *love* this quote from Marianne. Using her comparison of light to dark, that would mean that fear is simply the absence of love. In our current reality, these are a few of the countless behaviors that we often see when people choose to remain in the darkness, instead of stepping into the light:

» They fight fire with fire.
» They make excuses and blame others, while doing nothing to offer solutions.
» They use the recounting of troubling events on twenty-four-hour news channels as an excuse to further separate themselves from people who do not look like they do, think like they do, or pray like they do.

» They choose to judge an entire group of people (brown people, police officers, white people, LGBTQ people, Muslim people, etc.), based on the actions of a few.

All those actions are rooted in fear. This type of fear emerges from the lowest and most primitive part of our minds, and it will consistently push us toward equally primitive results (separateness, hate, hopelessness, and the like), if we let it. Most importantly, fear is not our natural state. We are social creatures who thrive on connection and, as many spiritual teachers have said, our natural state of being is love.

That is what Ubuntu and this journey to go together are all about. Love. Or, more specifically, *the courage to choose love.*

And even though love is our natural state, it is not always easy to behave in that manner. Here is what it looks like to consistently choose love over fear:

» Being peaceful and caring instead of impulsively resorting to violence.

» Seeking to understand—or, better yet, *hanging out with*— people who are different from you, so you can realize that you are really not that different from them after all.

» Raising the level of thoughtful discussion online, instead of being a "keyboard gangsta" by anonymously hurling hateful and ignorant comments at others like a coward.

» Diving headfirst into healing our world in any way possible, instead of leaving this hard work for someone else to do for you.

That is what love would do.
Is that what you would do, too?
That is what you need to answer, because here is the reality that is staring you in the face right now: *There is no one else who can spread this love except you.*

If you think that more hate, more separateness, more apathy, more guns, more excuses, more insensitivity, more name-calling, more victim-blaming, more hopelessness, and more violence are the answers to our problems, then you need to come to grips with the fact that you are part of the problem that many of us are working hard to fix.

And, yes, your fear is at the heart of it.

It is okay to be scared. As I noted earlier, I am scared, too. We live in a frightening world. But here's the deal—be scared if you need to be, but I'm desperately asking you to snap out of it as quickly as you can so that you can muster the courage to spread love and kindness as far and as wide as you can.

Love or fear—everything starts from one of those two places. That much, we already know.

The question that remains is this: *What are we going to do about it?*

Actually, don't answer that yet. Let's break down the two competitors in this age-old heavyweight battle so that you can make a better informed decision.

In One Corner, Introducing Fear

Contrary to what I mentioned earlier in this chapter, fear is not universally a bad thing.

Thankfully, it is the driving force that stops most people from doing incredibly dumb things, like juggling chain saws while blindfolded, wrestling grizzly bears during the next family camping trip, or jumping out of a third-story window while using a bedsheet as a parachute. Fear is an extremely useful emotion in some cases; without the evolutionary gift of having it hardwired into our brains, you and I (and the rest of the human race) would end up dead sooner than necessary.

While exercising caution and showing appropriate discretion are wonderful traits, using fear as the prime factor in *all* your decisions creates far more problems than it solves. If you let fear guide you when you want to ask your boss for a raise, walk away from an unhealthy relationship, begin a new creative pursuit, or—and this is the main message of this book—create meaningful connections with other human beings, then you are experiencing the worst of what fear has to offer. And, in these cases, fear becomes toxic, life-limiting, and, most of all, unnecessary.

So, what is fear? I view it as the anticipation of pain. The key word in the previous sentence is *anticipation*. And, as pointed out earlier, it makes sense to anticipate pain before you jump into shark-infested waters with raw steaks duct-taped to your body. But it makes far less sense to feel it before making a friendly connection with someone who may be different from you.

Worse still, have you noticed that, in most cases, we fear things that have not even happened yet? When we are driven by fear, we spend our precious energy shadowboxing with ghosts and other imaginary enemies in hopes of keeping ourselves safe. But safe from what, exactly?

Here are some examples of how fear has failed us:

» Fear is what drives bullying bosses to dehumanize their employees and systematically destroy their lives on a daily basis.
» Fear is what keeps people stuck in a mediocre existence, instead of pursuing their lifelong hopes and dreams before they die.
» Fear is what causes people to put walls around their heart to keep well-meaning people from getting too close (or, conversely, fear also keeps people stuck in soul-crushing relationships that they should have walked away from years ago).
» Fear is what inspires others to hate people who are different from them.
» Fear is the driving force behind every fight, war, form of abuse, and practically every atrocity that this world has ever seen.

» Fear is what will keep people from boldly standing up to a broken world by sharing love when no one else has the courage to do that.
» Let's unpack this a little bit. Thinking of those examples, what are they *really* afraid of?
» The bullying boss is afraid of the anticipated pain of losing control of her team.
» The man who chooses not to share his art with the world is afraid of the anticipated pain of looking foolish or having his creative expression rejected.
» The woman who builds walls around her heart is afraid of the anticipated pain of being emotionally hurt again (or, she stays in an unhealthy relationship because the anticipated pain of starting over outweighs the current pain of staying in the relationship).
» The man who hates people of other races, religions, or sexual orientations does so because (either through ignorance or misinformation) he anticipates the pain of these people negatively affecting his way of life in some way.
» The people who decide to resort to violence of any kind do so because they anticipate the pain of being attacked, so they choose to attack first.
» The people who choose not to love others anticipate the pain of pouring their heart and soul into the process of healing the world, only to potentially fail.

Did you notice something about all those fears? In every case, they are focused on what *could* happen. They are focused on pain that people *think* they will experience. But in every case, it has not happened yet. This is why—just as Marianne Williamson described the darkness—that fear is not a reality. Even though it might feel very real, it is something that resides solely in our imagination, so it is not real at all.

This is the secret and the truth about our fears.

This is why we must move with clarity when deciding to move forward with fear. Doing so is similar to stumbling around in the darkness, fighting against dragons that don't exist in order to protect us from threats that aren't even there—all while hurting ourself and others in the process.

Fear, the Killer

If you are more left-brained, let's get more practical. Do you know what living a fear-based life is doing to your health and well-being? It's not pretty.

Our bodies are built to react to stress and fear by releasing cortisol, which, in many circles, is known as the stress hormone. Of course, this is fine when you hear gunshots nearby or see a rabid dog rushing toward you, but if we remain in a constant state of heightened stress, our cortisol production stays locked in the on position. According to the Mayo Clinic, this can put us at an increased risk for a myriad of health issues, including:

» Anxiety
» Depression
» Digestive problems
» Headaches
» Heart disease
» Sleep problems
» Weight gain
» Memory and concentration impairment[2]

Psychology Today went as far as to call cortisol "Public Enemy No. 1."[3] And haven't you noticed that those who are driven by fear are not particularly joyful people?

You pay a price for constantly living in fear and suffering the stress that comes with anti-otherness. The fear that others are coming to take your job, take your joy, take your spouse, or take your way of life away from you could actually play a role in decreasing your overall health and well-being.

More specifically, staying in a fearful state will keep you isolated, prevent you from forming meaningful relationships, lead to more adversarial relationships, and may put you in the grave sooner than necessary. Worst of all, it's not even real!

Thankfully, there is another player in this battle.

In the Other Corner, Introducing Love

Love is a challenging topic to wrap your head around, mainly because there are so many forms of it. The Greeks used seven words to define these different forms of love:

> » *Storge*: Natural affection, the love you share with your family
> » *Philia*: The love you have for friends
> » *Eros*: Sexual and erotic love
> » *Agape*: Unconditional or divine love
> » *Ludus*: Playful love, like childish love or flirting
> » *Pragma*: Long-standing love (i.e., the love shared by a married couple)
> » *Philautia*: Love of the self[4]

Seems confusing, doesn't it? What is really confusing is that Americans simply use one word (*love*) to describe all of these concepts. That's probably why James, the former hospital administrator mentioned earlier in this chapter, was likely dismissed as a weirdo for signing off on his emails with "Love, James." The folks on the receiving end of his emails were likely thinking, "Wait, does this guy mean 'love' as a friend, or does he mean 'love-love'? Eww . . ."

The source of our confusion can be found in the dictionary. If you look there, you will find that *love* is defined as "an intense feeling of deep affection." Based on that definition, no wonder James's emails caused so much angst-ridden hand-wringing among his executive peers at the hospital where he formerly worked.

I have never connected with that definition because it doesn't feel as if it represents love in general. And I am sure that you know of at least a few people who claimed to have "intense feeling of deep affection" for their significant others or their children, and often expressed it in the form of extreme physical and emotional abuse. Sorry, but that is not love. Is love really love when we are not behaving lovingly? I certainly don't think so.

When I think of love, I don't view it as a capricious feeling that comes and goes inexplicably. Instead, there is more power in viewing love *as an action*. Unlike our feelings, which are often fleeting, our actions are always within our control. From the Ubuntu perspective, the purest form of love is not something we are waiting to feel; love is something we must do. *Now*, ideally.

So, what is love, then? I define it as "an active and steadfast dedication to the well-being and happiness of another." Working from this definition, it does not matter if you are referring to your children, your significant other, your best friend from college, the cheerful barista at Starbucks, the stranger sitting next to you on a cross-country flight, or the recipient of every email you send from now until the end of time—you can choose to literally love all of them.

When we are committed to the well-being and happiness of another person, we are kind, we are generous, we are helpful, we are respectful, we are forgiving, we are supportive, and, most of all, we are connected. Best of all, unlike fear (which is based on anticipated pain sometime in the future), behaving in a loving manner can only happen in the present— which is precisely why love is real.

Puppy Love and Oxytocin

Two months ago, I experienced the power of love and connection in action. My wife Amber and our daughters Kaya and Nia visited a magical place in Los Angeles called The Dog Café, which is a café that allows you to play with puppies and dogs who have been rescued from kill shelters. After we all enjoyed a hot cocoa, we were led into a room with a group of other folks, where we were all able to play for an hour with a bunch of rambunctious puppies and dogs, who were in search of a new home.

I lack the words to convey to you how much love was in that room for those sixty minutes, but I will try anyway. As the puppies jumped on us to play, they licked our faces, and one lovely chocolate lab puppy named Esther hopped immediately on my lap and then curled up into a ball and fell asleep. Our hearts nearly exploded with happiness. It is a miracle that we did not end up loading every single one of those puppies into my SUV and bringing them all back to our house.

On a deeper level, though, something else was happening in that room. All the people who were in the room were not only behaving in a loving manner toward the dogs and puppies in the room, but we were also more loving to each other as well. Before entering the room, all of us were strangers, but within minutes, as we played with the puppies, we were high-fiving each other, hugging each other, and instinctively behaving as if we were all long-lost friends. The action of loving the puppies inspired us to act lovingly toward each other, too. Afterward, I noticed that people emerging from the dog café were giving money to homeless folks on the way back to their cars and trading contact information with people they had only met a few minutes earlier. It was one of the most beautiful hours I have spent in my life, and the buzz from the love in the room stayed with me for days.

I had to learn more about that hour and what happened there from a scientific perspective. Dr. Eva Ritvo, a psychiatrist, internationally known speaker, and best-selling author, explained it beautifully in an article she wrote for *Psychology Today*:

> Oxytocin "the cuddle hormone" is among the most ancient of our neurochemicals and has a powerful effect on the brain and the body. When oxytocin begins to flow, blood pressure decreases . . . bonding increases, social fears are reduced and trust and empathy are enhanced.[5]

Whether we knew it or not, for that hour, we were all on an oxytocin high—and it was mind-blowing. As an added bonus, oxytocin has the power to counteract the life-limiting effects of cortisol, too.

You might be reading this and thinking, "So, are you suggesting that the next time that I'm not behaving in a loving manner, I should go play with a room full of puppies?!" *Yes, that's exactly what I'm saying.* But, in the spirit of practicality, if that is not possible, do the next best thing: Behave in a loving manner toward someone.

There are so many ways to do this. Perform a random act of kindness by committing to make someone's day, every day. Compliment good customer service instead of being the person who only speaks up when you receive poor service. Surprise a family member, a friend, or a colleague by saying how much you appreciate him or her. Encourage someone's dream, instead of listing all the reasons why it can't be done. Silently send out love to the people around you while you are waiting in line.

Think about when you have witnessed a loving act. Didn't it make you feel good? The beauty of loving actions is that they positively affect at least three people:

» The person offering the loving act
» The person receiving the loving act
» The person (or people) witnessing the loving act

Yes, acting in a loving manner has the power to improve our mood, our relationships, our health, and our connection to the world around us. Not to mention that it can also positively affect our faith in the unwavering goodness of humanity.

This is what happens if we choose to behave in a loving manner, and I believe that this is one of the best aftereffects of the Ubuntu mind-set.

It's Decision Time

So, what is it going to be, my friend? Love or fear? And, no, this is not a choice where you have the luxury of opting out.

Multiple times a day, every day, you will be placed at this fork in the road where you are forced to choose between fear and love. Whether it is in line at the grocery store, before you coach an employee, during a difficult conversation with a loved one, when you are choosing to connect with someone who is different from you in some way, before you vote in an upcoming election, or in your most private moments when you are determining what to do next, if you break it down to its simplest level, it always comes down to those two options.

You already know how I feel about this choice. As Marianne's quote at the beginning of the chapter states so clearly, *love is what we're born with*—so, love is what I will live with and die with. I have lived with fear long enough, and I have seen how it has failed me, my community, my country, and the world.

You already know this: Fearing each other is not the answer. If we choose to live together in the spirit of "I am, because we are," we must start by actively loving one another.

Unlike James's former peers, I know that there is nothing weird about love. If anything, what is strange is choosing to live, work, and lead without it.

CHAPTER 5

When Your Beliefs Become Irrelevant: The Unpleasant Reality behind Good Intentions

Your beliefs don't make you a better person;
your behavior does.

—Anonymous

This chapter is going to ruffle a few feathers. Well, at least, I hope it does.

To move to the Ubuntu mind-set of "I am, because we are," we are going to have to shift from how we have traditionally viewed the world. Last year, I shared with the readers of my website, *The Positivity Solution*, a story that played a role in shifting how I viewed what it means to live with positivity.

One Sunday morning on my way to the gym for my morning workout, I stopped by a nearby gas station to fill up my tank. Yes, if you are keeping score at home, this is the second time in this book where something noteworthy has happened to me on my way to the gym.

For some reason, I was not paying attention to the fact that the traffic light in front of me had just turned green as I stared blankly ahead at the road in front of me. As I sat in my daydream-induced stupor, I failed to notice that I was blocking a line of cars trying to exit from a nearby parking lot. And in true big-city fashion, within seconds, I was loudly reminded to move by a man who was trying to exit from that parking lot. He honked his horn excessively, and then rolled down his driver's-side window to address me directly.

"Hey, asshole, what in hell are you doing?! Move your damn car before I run your punk ass over!"

Whoa.

I was shocked. No, I wasn't shocked that he cursed at me (I live in Los Angeles, so that happens from time to time), or that his wife and his two young kids (presumably) were in the car and witnessed his mini-tirade.

I was shocked because that exchange took place as he was driving out of a church parking lot after Sunday service.

Your Beliefs Are No Longer Enough

Of course, there could be a myriad of reasons why the man in the car found it necessary to address me in that way. Perhaps he was in a desperate hurry to get somewhere. (Remain in curiosity, right?) More importantly, I have no interest in making broad and inaccurate judgments about churchgoers based solely on the actions of this man.

What this interaction did for me, though, was nudge me to look at this situation in a more meaningful way. And that interaction aligned with a troubling trend that is becoming more common in our world lately.

It's the idea that our beliefs alone matter.

This might be tough to hear, but to create a more connected world, our beliefs have minimal importance. It is the behavior we demonstrate *consistently* that has the power to positively change the world—not our beliefs.

Behavior, by definition, is the way we conduct ourselves—especially toward others. Cory Booker, a US senator from New Jersey, explains the difference between our beliefs and our behavior brilliantly in this quote:

> Before you speak to me about your religion, first show it to me in how you treat other people. Before you tell me how much you love your God, show me how much you love all His children. Before you preach to me of your passion for your faith, teach me about it through your compassion for your neighbors. In the end, I'm not as interested in what you have to tell or sell as in how you choose to live and give.[1]

I am not sure what was in that churchgoer's mind while he was cursing me out from his car with his family in tow, but I am going to guess that his behavior was not in line with the beliefs that were being discussed in the service he attended a few minutes earlier.

This is not about him, though. More importantly, as humans, aren't we all at least *a little guilty* of behaving in ways that run counter to our beliefs?

Consider these examples:

> » We believe that our families are our number-one priority, but we barely spend any meaningful time with our family members or tell them how much they mean to us.
> » We believe deeply in certain causes (e.g., caring for abused/ neglected children), but we do not devote any of our time or money to those causes.
> » We believe in kindness and positivity, but we consistently engage in mindless gossip about coworkers, we spend hours engaging in online battles in the comment section of social media posts, and we let our mood determine our manners.
> » We believe in making our health a priority, but we use our treadmill to hang our clothes.
> » We work in companies that believe in the lofty values that are posted in hallways, but they turn a blind eye to the harassment, bullying, and other atrocities occurring within their walls on a daily basis.

Let me ask you this: In any of those situations, do those beliefs *really* matter? I would say absolutely not. Hiding behind well-crafted and positive-sounding beliefs does nothing to move us closer to a more connected world.

I'll take this one step further. Notice that I said the behavior that we demonstrate *consistently* has the power to positively change the world. I did not say anything about *our actions*. Unfortunately, our actions don't always tell an accurate story about us, either.

Does it really matter if you go to church every Sunday, go to yoga three times a week and proudly say "Namaste" at the end of each session, or meditate on world peace each night before you go to bed, if you still consistently *behave* like a self-centered ass for the majority of your day?

You guessed it—*no*.

Going to church each week doesn't make someone a "good and kind person" any more than putting lettuce on my hamburger makes me a vegetarian. Our actions may look good on the surface, and they may even fool some people. But, in reality, it is only our behavior that positively or negatively affects the world we share.

And no matter how hard we may try, our consistent behavior is incapable of fooling anyone. It *always* tells the true story.

This is why, in order to connect our world, we are going to have to reject all forms of hypocrisy, and as best-selling author and leadership expert Robin Sharma once said, "make sure that your video is in sync with your audio."

The Beliefs That Destroy Connection (and What to Do about Them)

While our beliefs alone cannot do much, especially when they are not aligned with our behavior, sometimes our beliefs become the spark that fuels our behavior. In those cases, if they are not beliefs that foster connection, they can be extremely destructive. Here are three of those beliefs that can get in the way of Ubuntu:

1. The belief in better

Generally speaking, there is nothing wrong with believing that some things are better than others. For example, I will always think that the NCAA March Madness Tournament is better than every other sporting event on earth, that the Avengers are better than the Justice League (and could beat them in a fight), mid-1990s hip-hop is better than the current version, and white chocolate is better than milk chocolate. I am willing to debate all comers on those topics, by the way.

The "better" conversation becomes much more troubling when we start talking about human beings, and, unfortunately, there is research to support this. In 2016, researchers Ben Tappin and Ryan McKay published a study titled "The Illusion of Moral Superiority." In this study, participants were presented with a list of thirty traits, such as honesty, sincerity, warmth, likability, creativity, and the like. Then they were asked to rate (1) the extent to which they themselves displayed each of those traits, (2) how much the average person displayed each of those traits, and (3) the social desirability of each trait.

The study concluded that "most people strongly believe they are just, virtuous, and moral, yet regard the average person as distinctly less so."[2] This study's findings hit the nail on the head: Most people think they are better than the average person in many of those key areas (come on, you know that you do, too). It becomes dangerous when we begin to *behave* as if we're better than the average person.

Take a look at the following list and see if any of these people strike a nerve with you:

» The person who believes that his religion is better than other people's religions (or that he is better than people who choose not to follow any religion at all).

» The person who believes that she is better than people who wear uniforms to work (i.e., service professionals and waitstaff), and she goes out of her way to make that clear in every interaction with them.

» The person who believes that he is better than others based solely on superficial metrics, such as the zip code that he lives in, the car he drives, the college degree (or the number of them) he has earned, the size of his house, the number of social media followers he has amassed, or the money in his bank account.

» The person who believes that she is better than other employees in her company, solely because she wears a laminated badge that reads Director on it, and their badges do not.

» The person who believes that he is better than overweight people, because he is in flawless physical condition.

It is bad enough to believe these things, but once they morph into behaviors, they can hurt a lot of people. And since science confirms that many people believe they are already morally superior to those poor, downtrodden, average folks, it almost provides a justification to treat them in a less-than-kind manner.

The Ubuntu mind-set does not waste time with any of this foolishness. Since we are all connected in some way, how could I be better than anyone else? Splitting hairs and assigning gradations of awesomeness are merely ego-fueled exercises that widen the divide in our world, instead of closing it. It is time to start becoming curious and asking better questions.

What if your neighbor's religion was not the wrong way to worship, but simply another way to worship? What if you viewed every service employee as a skilled professional who is providing you with meaningful assistance, instead of someone to look down on? What if you viewed your fancy house, car, or college degrees not as a way to elevate yourself above others, but as something to be grateful for? What if you drew on your position as a director to serve as a mentor to those who may aspire to reach your level one day? What if you used the same dedication that gained you your perfect body to lovingly show others how you did it?

When we shift from being better to the connectedness of Ubuntu, we behave in a way that can heal our world.

2. The belief in colorblindness

Unlike the belief mentioned previously, for the most part, the belief in colorblindness usually comes from a good place. *Usually.* Either way, though, it doesn't make the end result any less destructive to the desired goal of meaningful connection.

Just to be clear, I am not referring to the problem faced by people who have a vision issue that makes it difficult for them to distinguish certain colors—that would make me a total jerk. I am referring to how people have been told that the polite thing to do is not to see our racial differences. Instead, people are often told to believe that the most beneficial thing they can do to create a more connected world is to be "blind" to other races and cultures. This is a very harmful lens through which to view the world.

I have lost count over the years of the number of times I was told by well-meaning people, "I don't see your race at all" or "I make a point not to see the color in other people." Each time, it caused a tiny piece of my soul to crumble to the ground because it implied that there is a part of me that would be better left unseen. If you do not see my color, my race, or my heritage, then how could you really see me?

I am Akinshola Mark Richards—the son of a West African man and a Mississippi woman, and I am very proud of that. My parents' stories, their struggles, their joys, and the uniqueness of their lives are inextricably woven into my life and have made me the man I am today. My life as an African-American man has also brought me my own stories, struggles, and joys—and I want you to see that. For us to connect in a meaningful way, *I need you to see that.*

The most damaging aspect of colorblindness is that it encourages us to put our collective heads in the sand and pretend that our differences do not exist, do not matter, or should not be discussed. None of which is true. The elephant in the room does not go away because we have chosen not to see that she's there.

When I think of the truest spirit of Ubuntu, it is about seeing our shared humanity—and celebrating all of it. Contrary to what some people may believe, we do not need to be the same or similar in order to connect deeply. In fact, I would argue that our connection becomes more meaningful by acknowledging (and, ideally, learning from) the differences of others.

It may be easier in the short term to view the world from a colorblind perspective and to avoid engaging in difficult discussions about race, but no one wins by taking the easy route in the long run. The only way out is through, and we can only become more united once we have the sometimes messy, emotional, and constructive conversations about our differences.

3. The belief in separateness

This is the belief that may have the greatest negative impact on us going together in a spirit of Ubuntu. Some people believe that the way to forge a better world is to create walls to protect their lives from other people who are not like them. Here are some of the examples of this that I have either read on social media or personally heard another person say to me during the past twelve months:

» "Black people are great as long as they're scoring touchdowns for my favorite team, singing songs that I enjoy, or serving me my food—but there will be a problem if one of them ever tries to date my daughter."

» "I'll be damned if I let a gay man be my son's second-grade teacher. They need to keep their perverted lifestyle at home and away from the classroom."

» "There is no way that I'm getting on a plane with a Muslim—ever."

» "No one is lazier than Mexicans. I won't make the mistake of hiring one ever again."

» "I would never rent out my house to foreigners."

Most would agree that these are not very enlightened views, but the reality is that certain people do harbor these kinds of beliefs and see nothing wrong with them at all. It is as if they were saying, "Look, there is nothing wrong with blacks, gays, Muslims, and foreigners, as long you keep them as far away from me, my family, and my life as possible."

But, as noted in the previous chapter, the need to stay separate is driven by fear, and fear is exactly what has gotten us into this mess. The rest of us will have to stay stuck in the current state of disconnection as long as the fearful fail to find the courage not to remain scared—which, in itself, is a pretty scary thought. The truth is that meaningful connection, going together, and living with a spirit of Ubuntu all become impossible to those who refuse to venture outside the walls of their fear-based comfort zones.

Assuming that this book has landed in the hands of a person who has chosen comfort over connection, I will use the remaining words of this chapter to speak directly to you.

I am not here to demonize you in any way. In many ways, I completely understand why you are scared, and why you feel that separation is the best way to keep you, your loved ones, and your way of life safe from harm. My hope is that you will consider an alternative way to view the world—and the view that I'm recommending is with a zoom lens.

It is easy to prejudge, be scared of, and hate others from far away. But, from personal experience, I know how much harder it is to do those things up close. If there is some aspect of the world that upsets you or that you want to change, I can promise you that your power to do anything positive is diminished as you sit behind your walls. My challenge to you is simple: Step outside your walls and shrink the distance between you and what you fear, or even hate. This may sound obvious, but it is impossible to fix whatever it is that you hate by throwing more hate at it.

More importantly, once you face what you fear, its power over your life decreases. I want you to experience a world where you look at the differences of others and do not feel fear or the need to run away and separate yourself from them. I want you to live fully. I want you to experience all that life has to offer, instead of the smaller version that you have settled for. I want you to realize that, despite our differences, you will also notice that we have many similarities. I want you to play an active role in healing our world.

Most of all, I want to connect with you and show you that the world's collective love can offer you so much more than your solitary fear—if you let it.

All that I need you to do is to take the first step.

This chapter is all about the importance of the right beliefs. I want you to know that I believe in you, my friend.

CHAPTER 6

You Belong in Any Room You Walk Into: The Importance of Healing Yourself First

You have been criticizing yourself for years, and it hasn't worked. Try approving of yourself and see what happens.

—Louise Hay

As a child, I was bullied for having very crooked teeth (thank God for braces—which I wore as a kid and then again as an adult), and for struggling with a stutter throughout my younger days. Standing out is great if you are a famous musician or a world-class professional athlete, but as a kid in elementary school? Not so much.

Maya Angelou's wise words were very true: "I've learned that people will forget what you said, people will forget what you did, but people will never forget how you made them feel." The teasing and name-calling haunted me, and, as a forty-three-year-old man, I can still remember how it made me feel when I was ridiculed, excluded, and made to feel like a freak on a near-daily basis. And even though I was not aware of it, the feelings of inadequacy followed me throughout my athletic pursuits, romantic relationships, and professional endeavors as I grew into adulthood.

The annoying feeling that kept needling me for decades was that *there was something wrong with me, and once that was discovered, no one would want to be around me.*

In basketball, I thought that I was selected for the team because of my athleticism and because I looked the part as a tall and slender guy—not because I was particularly skilled. In all my romantic relationships, I feared that the women who chose to date me only did so until they found someone who was more handsome, intelligent, and interesting. At work, I spent days in quiet terror as I feared the day that I would be found out as a fraud who didn't know what he was doing much of the time.

Looking back on it now, it is so easy to see the pattern of dysfunctional thinking, but, as I was living through it, I was blind to all of it.

Everything changed for me on that fateful day thirteen years ago when my abysmally low self-esteem, combined with the relentless workplace bullying I was dealing with, fueled my attempt to take my own life (the details of that harrowing episode are spelled out in my previous book, *Making Work Work*, so I won't rehash them here). That was the lowest point of my life, but I am intensely thankful for it because it forced me to finally take charge of my life and embark on the challenging road to emotional recovery. Believe me, it is amazing how quickly you can get your act together when death is staring you in the face (not that it is a recommended strategy to do so), and that is exactly what I did.

Once my mind cleared, I realized something that is painfully obvious to most people, but eluded me until I was in my thirties: *You cannot engage in a healthy relationship unless you love yourself first.*

Or, worded differently, before you go together in the spirit of Ubuntu, be sure to heal yourself first.

In this chapter, I want to make sure that you bring your best self before you choose to go together with anyone. As you have read in the previous five chapters, healing our world is going to be hard work, and now is the time to focus that hard work on ourselves. All of it will be based on this simple mantra, which I wish I knew decades ago:

You belong in any room that you walk into.

Why Self-Love Must Be Priority Number One

I want you to picture this completely fictional scenario in your mind, if you can:

A mother is teaching her five-year-old daughter how to tie her own shoes for the very first time. Despite the little girl's best efforts, after a few minutes or so, she is unable to successfully tie her shoes. The mother looks at her daughter with extreme disappointment, and with palpable disdain dripping off every word, she locks eyes with her daughter before she unloads on her: "You are such an idiot. What in the hell is wrong with you? You'll never amount to anything. You're pathetic." Immediately after hearing those words from her mother, tears well up in the little girl's eyes as she runs away into her room and sobs uncontrollably into her pillow.

Okay—scenario over.

That was horrific, wasn't it? Even though you knew that the scenario was completely fictional, I'll bet it stirred up some emotions in you. The idea that a mother would speak to her kindergarten-aged child in such a vicious manner—especially since she was trying her best—is almost impossible to imagine.

Here's the thing, though—*I'll bet that you have said those words to yourself, or worse, when you have messed up, even though you tried your best, haven't you?* And unlike the made-up story with the mother and her child, when you speak to yourself like that, it is for real.

Sadly, we often reserve a special kind of viciousness for ourselves that we would never dream of spewing at another person—and we cannot afford to engage in this destructive indulgence if we want to heal the world by going together. When we do not see ourselves as lovable or worthy of love, we are traveling the on-ramp to this vicious cycle. Maybe you have experienced it before, because I know I have.

» When you do not direct love and kindness to yourself, that often leads to your minimizing or dismissing the love and kindness that is being offered to you by others.

» Because you see yourself as unworthy of love and kindness, you view the people who are trying to extend love and kindness to you as dumb, pathetic, or as damaged goods (only a loser would choose to love you, right?), and then you actively or unconsciously sabotage the relationship.

» Finally, you end up being around people who consistently treat you poorly because that treatment aligns with how you feel about yourself—which only further reinforces the negative feelings you have about yourself.

I cannot say this more definitively—going together with someone who does not value you, respect you, or care about you is *far worse* than going alone.

The only way out of this vicious cycle is to cultivate self-love. Yes, I know that term has been so overused that it has almost lost its meaning, but without the ability to be compassionately loving toward ourselves during this crazy journey called life, we will always fall short of our highest potential.

In Chapter 4, I talked about viewing love as something we *do*, as opposed to something we feel. This is especially true of self-love. When we think of what compassionate people do for us, we see that they offer words of encouragement when we stumble, they give us a shoulder to cry on when we are sad, they notice our best traits and appreciate them, they comfort us when we are scared, they provide a safe space for us to be ourselves, and, consistently, they love and accept us for who we are. All those things, and many more, are what we must do for ourselves on a daily basis.

Similar to the love that was mentioned in Chapter 4, we do not have to wait until we feel that we are worthy of this love to *behave* as if we are worthy of it—which we always are. As with most meaningful things, it will take action to get us there, and here is that specific action: *We must speak to ourselves with the same love and kindness we would direct toward the person we love the most on this earth.*

And, as a rule of thumb, before you say anything to yourself, ask yourself, "Is this how I would communicate to a loved one?" If you paused to ask yourself that critically important question on a day-to-day basis—or, better yet, on a moment-to-moment basis—just imagine how much better your life would become. You should begin this soul-nourishing habit today and practice it consistently.

When I first started writing *Go Together*, it was not coming *together* as fast as I would have liked (I am sure there's a joke in there somewhere). After another failed writing session at the beginning of this project, I launched into a mean-spirited attack that was directed at my writing struggles.

"Really, Shola? You've been working on this book for a month now and all you have written is a little over a thousand words?! You are pathetic, man. Get your act together before your publisher regrets ever giving you the deal to write this book." Looking back on it now, there must be something about the solitary process of writing a book that brings out this kind of cruel self-talk, because I had a similar conversation when I was writing my previous book.

Thankfully, I interrupted this destructive pattern by thinking about my two elementary school–aged daughters, Kaya and Nia. How would I respond to them if they were struggling with an important project? On my worst day, I would never dream of speaking to them in the manner in which I had just addressed myself, that is for sure. So, I tried speaking to myself with the same sort of love and compassion that I would offer them—and I actually spoke to myself out loud. Here is what I said:

"It's all good, Shola! Be patient with yourself. I know it's hard now, but if you keep showing up and trying your best, it will get easier. Don't beat yourself up, man. You're a talented writer and I believe in you and your message. You belong in every room that you walk into, and you are built for this. Keep moving forward, and I'll be here to support you every step of the way."

Big difference, right? I know this is easy to dismiss as some new-agey mumbo jumbo, but I cannot overstate the power of this simple exercise. Ever since that conversation I had with myself, I made a point of writing this book with a picture of my daughters nearby, and that has increased my productivity tenfold by gently reminding me to give myself the kind of love I would give to them whenever I fall short—which, like most humans, is fairly often.

The most important words on this earth will always be the words that we say about ourselves *to* ourselves.

This is the love that will allow us to go together.

The Impostor Club

Another sneaky way that we are unkind to ourselves is by minimizing our skills and accomplishments. This needs to be addressed immediately, because if you do not feel as if you belong in every room you walk into, that could delay—or, outright, stop you—from making the connections to heal this world.

Have you ever felt the sinking feeling that you have been fooling everyone into thinking you are better, smarter, and more qualified than you really are? If so, there's an official name for this phenomenon.

This insidious mind virus is known as the Impostor Syndrome, and here's an excellent definition of it, courtesy of the magazine *Fast Company*:

> Impostor syndrome is a psychological phenomenon in which people are unable to see their own accomplishments, dismissing them as luck, timing, or as a result of deceiving others into thinking they are more intelligent and competent than they believe themselves to be.[1]

The good news is that if you are thinking you are alone in feeling like a fraud—you are not. I am right there with you, as are countless others who struggle to believe that they belong in the room they are currently in.

Two years ago, I was invited to be a speaker on an author panel at a very large conference. Specifically, I was on a panel with five extremely gifted authors who were there to talk about their books to a large audience of librarians. Predictably, since I was the only first-time author selected for the panel, the Impostor Syndrome was raging out of control in my mind before the event started. In hopes of doing something to calm the flock of vultures swirling around in my stomach (Read: Distract me from throwing up all over myself), I decided to strike up a conversation with the other authors while we were waiting for the event to begin.

"Out of curiosity, since I'm a newbie to this author stuff—what was the hardest aspect for you in writing your books?" I asked with sincere interest in their answers.

"Oh, without question it's the self-doubt," one author said immediately. "I would sit at my computer for hours typing up something, only to read it over and realize that it was a steaming pile of crap. Then I would go to my room, curl up into the fetal position with a bottle of wine, and cry about how much of a fraud I was until the tears stopped. Then I would dry my tears, crawl back to my computer, and start typing again. That was the process that I repeated until my book was finally done."

All the other authors on the panel instantly chimed in.

"Yes! That is *so* me!" One of the authors enthusiastically blurted out.

"Whoa, here I was thinking that I was the only one who did that," another author said with stunned amazement.

"I feel so much better knowing that I'm not alone!" another author said with a sigh of relief.

To say that I was completely blown away by this conversation would be the understatement of the year. As embarrassing as this is to admit, I honestly felt that I was the only person who was consumed by the Impostor Syndrome as I was writing my book. I could not have been more wrong.

I was not an impostor, and I did belong in that room and on that panel.

According to the *Fast Company* article I cited earlier, over 70 percent of people have experienced the Impostor Syndrome at one time or another in their lives. The 70 percent undoubtedly includes famous movie stars, professional athletes, Grammy-winning musicians, leaders of countries, *New York Times* best-selling authors, the CEOs of Fortune 500 companies, and the guy/gal you keep seeing at the coffee shop and have a crush on, just to name a few.

On a positive note, that means that you and I are in very good company. More importantly, though, this is a wonderful reminder that feeling inadequate from time to time is a normal and expected part of being human.

Also, now that you are aware of this, I hope that it will no longer serve as an excuse not to move forward.

Eliminating Comparison

Speaking of feeling inadequate, very few habits bring on this feeling as effectively as needless comparison to others. And nothing inspires this habit more than social media. Don't get me wrong: I don't think there is anything inherently evil about social media. In fact, I believe that it was created to help us connect to other people all over the world in ways that were not possible before its existence. However, in many ways, I also believe that social media has encouraged many of us to feel more disconnected from the world by inspiring us to compare ourselves to our friends', family's, and even complete strangers' lives, multiple times a day.

Take a minute to put down this book and open up the social media apps on your smartphone. As you swipe through your newsfeed, what do you see?

» One of your friends posted a picture with her new boyfriend having a romantic dinner, captioned, "I am *so* in love with this guy! He's perfect!"
» Another one of your friends just finished running a half-marathon for her fortieth birthday, and posted a picture showing off her six-pack abs, with the hashtag: #ageisjustanumber.
» Another friend shared an update that he just landed his dream job, making six figures a year.

» Another friend took a picture of his perfect family, who are all smiles, as they are about to board a plane for yet another exotic family vacation.

How would you feel seeing those accomplishments if you are currently sitting at home in a less-than-perfect relationship (or no relationship at all), too tired from working long hours in a job that you despise to go to the gym—much less run a half-marathon—or whose family life is full of drama, bickering, and stress?

I am guessing that you would feel disconnected from those people, and that is exactly what I am trying to avoid. Comparison is one of the most common forms of self-cruelty, because it creates division between you and others, it erodes your self-esteem, it makes you believe that you don't belong in the room you are figuratively walking into, and, worst of all, what you are comparing yourself to isn't even real.

This should not be surprising to you, but the information that you see from your friends on Facebook, Instagram, or any other social media site is not anywhere close to the real world. What you are viewing is a heavily edited highlight reel. It does not matter who it is, it is close to impossible for anyone's normal, everyday life to measure up against anyone's highlight reel.

We often compare our complete stories (including our ups and downs, failures and insecurities) to the incomplete—and often perfectly edited—stories that we see from others on Facebook. No wonder it is so easy to feel down in the dumps after spending any significant time on social media. If you fall into the trap of comparing your life to what you see online, your vacations will never be as mind-blowing as your coworkers' vacations, your relationship will never be as romantic and loving as your friends' relationships, your kids will never be as well-behaved as your neighbors' kids, and you will never achieve the happiness and peace that everyone on your newsfeed is enjoying, except you.

But none of that is true.

Comparing yourself to others is a recipe for unhappiness, but comparing yourself to a world that isn't even real has the power to destroy your sanity.

Self-Care Is Ubuntu

Imagine if you were going on a road trip from New York City to Los Angeles, and you wanted to arrive at your destination as quickly as possible. Would you ever say to yourself, "I am too busy driving to stop and refuel—I won't let anything stop me from getting to my destination!" If so, good luck when you eventually run out of gas and break down on the side of the freeway, and your goal becomes indefinitely delayed.

Of course, no one would ever do that while driving across the country. Yet, we often do this in our everyday lives. And that will eventually lead us toward a breakdown that could be far worse than anything that could happen to our cars. This is where self-care comes in.

Many times when I mention the importance of self-care, I am met with eye rolls and with a dismissive "Yeah, yeah . . . I know this already" wave of the hand. If you do already know this, that is fantastic. But, more importantly, are you actually doing it? Your answer holds the key to whether you will be able to sustain going together in a spirit of Ubuntu.

When I think of the phrase "I am, because we are," I believe that we must emphasize the "I am" part to ensure that we are serious about bringing our best selves to the togetherness equation. This means that our body, mind, and our spirit must be treated with reverence to ensure that we are healthy enough to create healthy relationships with others. Nourish it consistently with good books, meditation, and proper sleep; minimize your consumption of news; distance yourself from toxic friends and acquaintances who drain you; take regular vacations; eat nutrient-rich foods; take walks and do other forms of exercise; but, most of all, make a personal commitment to do these things, and anything else that will fully prepare you for the arduous road ahead.

You already know that to step into your role of healing the world, you cannot do it as a burned-out, exhausted, cortisol-fueled stress case. Our disconnected and damaged world needs you at your best right now, and that starts with the love and care that you are willing to give yourself. The confidence you gain from consistent self-care will come in handy as you wage the constant battles between self-doubt and self-esteem, fear and love, separateness and togetherness.

This begins with the steadfast realization that you deserve the love and kindness that you are directing toward yourself. Despite what you may believe, you are not lazy if you choose to take a vacation from work; you are giving yourself the rest and renewal that your mind and body needs to perform optimally. You are not selfish for saying "no" to the person who only reaches out to you when she needs something; you are enforcing healthy boundaries. You are not a bad person if you choose to separate yourself from a family member who consistently brings you drama, toxicity, and pain; you are protecting yourself, your happiness, and your sanity.

The problem is that when we do not make self-care and self-love a priority—or worse, when we act as if we don't deserve those things—we are unable to see the truth in any of those situations. This is an all-too common mistake, and it is not one that we can afford to make any longer as we do this important work.

My final plea to you in this part of the book is simple: We cannot effectively live together or go together as broken individuals. We will always be imperfect, but we cannot allow our imperfections and insecurities to stop us from moving forward for a moment longer. All those you have ever admired have transformed the world—or your world—in spite of what was holding them back. It is time for us to learn from their example.

The good news is that our insecurities and fears are not things that we are feeling alone. We are in this together, and that is the beauty of realizing that you are not in this by yourself. I am here for you, and you are here for me, and together we can be here for the world that we live in.

Move with confidence and know that you belong in any room you walk into, now, tomorrow, and always.

PART THREE

WORK TOGETHER

CHAPTER 7

Becoming the Hero: Why You Must Start Before You're Ready

If you don't require the journey to be easy, comfortable or safe, you can change the world.

—Seth Godin

could hear the naysayers' voices in my mind when I decided to dedicate one part of this book to creating a spirit of Ubuntu in our workplaces.

"Get real, Shola. Getting people to embrace an idea of 'I am, because we are' in our hypercompetitive, every-man-for-himself workplaces will never work."

Those words are familiar to me because they are the exact ones that were directed toward me before my first book, *Making Work Work*, was published. I was literally laughed at by colleagues, friends, former professors, and even complete strangers when I told them that I was writing a book about starting a movement to bring kindness, respect, and civility back to the modern workplace. I often wonder if they are still laughing now.

Shortly after *Making Work Work* was released, I was blown away by the emails and in-person testimonials from readers who took action by starting "positivity movements" in their workplaces.

Using the techniques in the book, everyday men and women did extraordinary things. Some successfully got long-tenured bullying bosses removed from their positions; others set firm boundaries when they were on the verge of becoming burned out or having a nervous breakdown; and still others even transformed highly toxic work environments into healthy, respectful, and productive ones. In each of those cases, overcoming those challenges probably seemed impossible at first, but as the late Nelson Mandela once said, "It always seems impossible until it's done."

I did notice something interesting about their stories, though. The overwhelming majority of the emails or comments that I received from my readers had two themes in common:

1. They did not initially believe that someone like them (i.e., an individual with no authority in the organization) could make a meaningful, positive difference in their workplace.

2. They underestimated how hard it was going to be to make meaningful, long-term, positive change in their workplace.

Those are the two key points that I want to focus on in this chapter. You may not feel as if you are ready to bring the Ubuntu philosophy into the workplace and inspire your colleagues to go together. You may also be intimidated by the potential roadblocks and obstacles that are lying in wait for you if you choose to make your work department or your organization more connected. Both are okay. What is not okay is allowing those things to stop you.

Consider this chapter as my attempt to psych you up for the difficult road that lies ahead. The journey to reinvent our workplaces based on the Ubuntu philosophy will not likely be easy, comfortable, or safe—there is no sense in denying this. Seth Godin's quote at the start of this chapter is the map that we will begin with, as we address each of those needs one by one so that you can effectively become one of the heroes who will heal the working world.

Even if you don't believe that you are ready.

．．

I have never in my life envied a human being who led

an easy life. I have envied a great many people who led

difficult lives and led them well.

—*Theodore Roosevelt*

．．

1. The need for it to be easy

Do you remember the Ubuntu story with the African children that I told at the beginning of Chapter 2? That is the story I use to kick off my keynote speeches as well. I cannot think of a better story to simply, but effectively, explain the power of Ubuntu and the African proverb "If you want to go fast, go alone. If you want to go far, go together." When I personally heard that powerful Ubuntu story for the first time years ago, I could not wait to get onto a stage to share the brilliance of that story with an audience—and three weeks after I had heard the story for the first time, I finally had my chance.

I was invited to speak to a group of nurses who were dealing with some severe interpersonal challenges (peer-to-peer bullying, backbiting, gossip, and the like), and the director of the unit wanted me to speak to them in hopes of inspiring positive change. *Perfect!* I had my Ubuntu story fully rehearsed and ready to be unleashed. It was time to change some lives!

Once I was onstage, I enthusiastically shared the Ubuntu story with the nurses—and I even yelled, "Ubuntuuuuuuuuuuuu!" at the top of my lungs for five seconds straight as an added finishing touch, in hopes of driving home the power of this life-altering word to the audience. Once I finished, I figuratively buffed my fingernails on the lapel of my suit and waited for wild applause to fill the room.

That applause never came.

Instead, I was met with a combination of curious, tilted-head stares that are often directed at exotic zoo animals, muffled laughter, intense secondhand embarrassment that forced some nurses to cover their eyes with their hands, and a twinge of disgust. Needless to say, that was not what I was going for.

One nurse, who clearly chose the disgust option after hearing my story, broke the awkward silence by eviscerating me while I stood helplessly onstage.

"Cute story, Shilo, or whatever your name is, but we're not in Africa, okay? What do you want me to do? If there is a nurse-manager opening, should I grab my competition's hand as we joyfully skip to the computer to apply for the same position together? I can see it now—we can even chant 'Ubuntu! Ubuntu! Ubuntuuuuuuuu!' as we do it, too. Give us a break. We're dealing with real problems, and your plan to help us is to come here and scream made-up African words at us?! Give us strategies that actually work!"

Ouch.

She did have a point, though. While I absolutely love the story, what good is that story without a strategy to make it real? Ever since that humiliating experience, I developed a strategy to bring the Ubuntu philosophy to life in a work setting (see Chapter 8). More immediately, the nurse's comment was the wake-up call that I needed to remind me that introducing the power of the Ubuntu in a professional setting is not going to be an easy undertaking.

Embracing the Challenge of Creating Ubuntu at Work

As I have noted numerous times throughout this book, Ubuntu is translated as "I am, because we are." In essence, it reflects the ultimate in teamwork, connectedness, and selflessness. Unfortunately, those words do not often describe how we work in America.

In many workplaces in America, separateness and hypercompetitiveness are not things to be avoided—they are often encouraged as the exact strategies necessary to survive or get ahead. Below are a few of the countless examples of how this works. I am sure you will not have to dig too deeply in your own professional history for a time when you experienced one of the following:

» The coworker who consistently steals credit for your work
» The boss who will throw you under the bus for a botched project, especially if it means that he can avoid shouldering any of the blame for the failure

» The guy who does not give a second thought to how his attitude and behavior affect his customers or the other members of the team

» The woman who shows up to work and does nothing but watch cat videos on YouTube, and turn oxygen into carbon dioxide for eight hours

If you believe in separateness, it is easy to do those things, and far worse, at work. More frighteningly—when people are not engaged at work, it becomes even easier to stay disconnected. Unfortunately, the latest statistics in that regard are not promising. According to research compiled by OfficeVibe.com:

» 13% of employees are engaged worldwide (seriously, let that paltry percentage sink in for a moment)

» 42% of employees feel that the leadership in their organization does not contribute to a positive company culture

» 51% of workers are looking to leave their current jobs[1]

In case you are wondering, I am not sharing these statistics to scare you. I am sharing them with you so that you are fully aware of what you will be up against if you choose to join me in creating kinder, more positive, and more connected workplaces, based on the Ubuntu philosophy. Before I can get to the strategies in the next chapter, it is important to address the issues that may stop you before you attempt to try them.

And one of the biggest issues is giving up because the journey won't be easy.

The unpleasant reality is that none of this will be easy. Now that we have that out of the way, let's focus on a more important question: Do we really need it to be easy in order to take action? Nothing that will maximize our potential while we are on earth is going to be easy. Don't believe me?

> » Ask a person who made the agonizing decision to permanently walk away from a toxic relationship with a family member.
> » Ask a single, working mom who found the time to accomplish her lifelong dream of getting a college degree while raising two little boys.
> » Ask a person who mustered the discipline to make better food choices, kept showing up at the gym, even though he was severely overweight, and, as a result, lost seventy pounds and fully regained his health.
> » Ask a person who found the courage to stand up to an abusive boss who was making her life a living hell.
> » Ask a person who looked at his paralyzing fear of public speaking square in the eyes and gave a successful presentation in front of one hundred complete strangers.

One thing you will never hear any of them say was that it was *easy*. I would put positively transforming the working world in the same category. This will be hard work, and to achieve the success we seek, we must embrace the challenge. If these things were easy, everyone would be doing them. But they're not easy, and everyone is not doing them because *they're hard as hell.* In some cases, these things might be the hardest things you will ever do in your life.

Actually, scratch that.

The hardest thing you will ever do in your life is making the life-destroying decision to *only* do what is easy. It may not seem that way now, but if you choose that road, there will come a day when you will look back with intense regret on a passed-up opportunity to heal a working world desperately in need of connection.

And trust me, that won't be easy to deal with.

....

A man grows most tired while standing still.

—*Chinese Proverb*

....

2. The need to be comfortable

You are not here on this earth to be comfortable.

You are here to grow into the greatest life that you possibly can live, and, ideally, inspire others to do the same. Just like most things that require growth—whether it is learning something new, maintaining a healthy lifestyle, sharing your art with the world, or honoring your boundaries— it cannot be done without some measure of discomfort.

This is especially true when it comes to choosing to live out the Ubuntu philosophy at work. For the people who are used to clawing their way up the corporate ladder, blowing out others' candles to make theirs shine brighter, and putting themselves first at all costs, this will be quite an uncomfortable shift. More importantly, though, it will also be uncomfortable for you to introduce this new way of thinking to them.

Sadly, though, most humans opt to remain comfortable (or pretend that they are comfortable) rather than to willingly step into discomfort by making a necessary change. I know that I am pulled toward choosing the temptation of comfort over choosing the temporary pain of growth on a daily basis.

I believe that we almost always know the right thing to do. You know that you should choose the veggies over the French fries when you are dining out. You know that you should be giving your children attention instead of responding to work emails on the weekend. You know that you should have that long-overdue conversation with your coworker who is not fulfilling his responsibilities on the team project. Unfortunately, knowing what to do in those cases means nothing if you have decided that staying comfortable with inaction is more appealing than your growth.

But keep in mind that your life will be severely limited if comfort is the main deciding factor in how you live. By consistently opting for comfort, you will not embrace Ubuntu, you will not reach out to people who are different from you, and you will not challenge others who believe that separateness is the answer—because all those things are guaranteed to be uncomfortable.

Comfort is glorious if you are fortunate enough to find it on a cramped, cross-country flight while stuck sitting in the middle seat—but as the default mode for living your life, it is unquestionably one of the worst strategies ever.

Thankfully, there is a better way.

Being Comfortable with Being Uncomfortable

Have you have heard the phrase that "life happens outside your comfort zone"? From my experience, that is the absolute truth.

The need to stay comfortable deadens our life experience. If we never travel outside our hometown, never try anything that could make us look silly, never try a new exercise regimen, never try unfamiliar foods, or would never consider dating a person outside of our race or religion, we are risking so much more than merely missing out on all that life has to offer. *We are risking becoming numb to our daily experience.*

If each person, each place, or each experience is largely similar to the people and places you experience every day of your life, it becomes easier to drift into autopilot mode and lose the wonder, joy, and appreciation of simply being alive. Comfort requires very little of your attention and effort; discomfort, on the other hand, requires both.

If you are trying to communicate with the locals in a foreign country, pushing through a challenging workout, having your first telephone conversation with someone you would like to date, or hopping onstage at a karaoke bar for the first time, you cannot sleepwalk through any of those situations. Your discomfort forces you to be present, and being present is the most effective way to move through life and experience it at its fullest.

It is worth remembering that everything that is currently comfortable for you was likely uncomfortable for you at one point: driving a car, using a computer or your smartphone, changing your baby's diapers, speaking a foreign language, or programming your DVR. But you stuck with it despite your discomfort, and your inevitable reward was growth.

I want you to remember that as we move into bringing the Ubuntu philosophy into our workplaces. We cannot grow when we are comfortable.

....

It is impossible to live without failing at something, unless

you live so cautiously that you might not have lived at

all—in which case, you fail by default.

—*J. K. Rowling*

....

3. The need to play it safe

Whenever I think of the luminaries who positively changed the world throughout history, it is easy to think of them as larger-than-life superhumans, never experiencing fear, insecurities, and the other unpleasantness of being mortal.

Nelson Mandela. Martin Luther King Jr. Mahatma Gandhi. William Shakespeare. The Dalai Lama. Rosa Parks. Mother Teresa. Albert Einstein. Anne Frank. Leonardo Da Vinci. Malala Yousafzai. The list goes on and on.

These people are equal parts inspiring and intimidating to me. On the one hand, I look at their intelligence, courage, and leadership skills and I aspire to have a similar positive impact on the world. On the other hand, I look at their intelligence, courage, and leadership skills and my insecurities remind me that I am light-years away from even coming close to having the positive impact that they have had on the world.

Whether I am inspired or intimidated, I recognize that the positive trait that they all share is that none of those men and women chose to play it safe. They shared their art with the world. They stared down their oppressors. They fought for what they believed in. And, most importantly, as a result, their positive impact on the world will likely be felt forever.

You might think that this is crazy, but *that is exactly what I want for you.*

There is no need to look over your shoulder—yes, I am talking directly to you. I want you to think and dream bigger than you may be accustomed to thinking in order to get results that you may not be accustomed to seeing. It is not as if Martin Luther King Jr. shot out of his mother's womb like a heat-seeking missile and landed on the steps of the Lincoln Memorial in Washington, D.C., ready to deliver his iconic "I Have a Dream" speech. He was a regular man who grew up with the same fears, the same imperfections, and the same doubts that you and I have. There is one difference between us and him, though, and it is a big one.

He gave up the need to play it safe.

Are you willing to do the same?

Your Safety Is an Illusion

Take a moment to reread the quote from J. K. Rowling on the previous spread. It is one of my favorite quotes of all time because it destroys the illusion of safety. In essence, she astutely provides us with only two options:

1. Attempt to achieve your goals, hopes, and dreams, and risk failure while doing so.

2. Live (if you want to call it that) a small, confined, risk-free life until you eventually die—a life in which you will fail by default.

Given that there really is no choice that will guarantee you eternal safety, option 2 seems to be a far riskier path to take, doesn't it? More urgently, though, you are noticing that the current state of the world is becoming more divided, our workplaces are becoming more disengaged, and people in general are feeling unhappier and more disconnected from each other than ever before, right? How does playing it safe help you, or anyone else, to fix any of this?

The world needs you as an active player in this game, my friend. Think of it this way: What if nothing in your workplace, your life, or the world changed for the rest of your life? If you are fine with that, then you probably do not need this book. However, if you are like me, and that is a reality that scares the hell out of you, you have only one choice available to you:

Do something about it.

Your health, your career, your relationships, your results, your well-being, and your impact on the world all depend on your ability to abandon the need to be safe. And hopefully, by now, you know that your safety is an illusion anyway.

I wish I could tell you that the road ahead will be easy, comfortable, and safe, but I can't do that. Then again, what would be the fun in that? This is about being the hero that your workplace and the world desperately needs, and I believe that this book is in your hands because you want to embrace the challenge. You may not feel confident or ready—I am not ready, either, but I am still here. Thankfully, our confidence and readiness are not requirements to begin.

Remember, we are in this together. Next, we will jump into the Ubuntu master plan that will provide us with the necessary structure to start the process of healing our workplaces.

Ready or not, hero, the world is waiting for you.

CHAPTER 8

The Master Plan:
Eight Keys to Unlocking
Ubuntu at Work

*No matter how brilliant your mind or strategy, if you're
playing a solo game you will always lose out to a team.*

—Reid Hoffman

During the 2006–2007 NBA season, the Boston Celtics, by all objective accounts, were a horrendous basketball team.

By the end of the 2007 season, the once-proud basketball franchise that had won sixteen NBA championships was reduced to a bumbling and inept shell of their former greatness. They finished with a record of twenty-four wins and an abysmal fifty-eight losses, which ranked them twenty-ninth out of thirty teams in the entire league that season—only the Memphis Grizzlies (twenty-two wins and sixty losses) had a worse year. Admittedly, as a lifelong fan of the Los Angeles Lakers—the longtime rival to the Celtics—the sorry state of their franchise pleased me greatly, and my soul reveled in the schadenfreude.

Then something big happened.

In the summer of 2007, after their failed season came to a merciful end, the Boston Celtics decided to make some major changes to their team. Specifically, they acquired two perennial All-Star players—Ray Allen and Kevin Garnett—to join the Celtics' franchise superstar, Paul Pierce, to create what was known as the Big Three. Believe it or not, as big as that move was, that was not the "something big" that I was referring to earlier.

Glenn "Doc" Rivers—the head coach of the Celtics at the time—wisely realizing that he needed to get these three superstars to work together, decided to introduce the team to a word and a philosophy that you are already familiar with by now: *Ubuntu.*

Throughout the following season, in 2007–2008, the new-look Celtics enthusiastically shouted "Ubuntu!" after they broke from every huddle, as a reminder that to reach their fullest potential as a team, their collective success would have to take priority over individual achievements. This was a huge shift for the newly formed Big Three, each of whom had enjoyed enormous individual success as the unquestioned best player on their former teams just a year ago. Significant individual sacrifices were made as everyone on the Celtics embraced their new team philosophy, and the results were nothing less than astonishing.

At the end of the 2007–2008 regular season, they finished with sixty-six wins and only sixteen losses, which was not only the best record in the entire league, but at the time of this writing is still the greatest single-season turnaround in NBA history. Even more impressively, armed with their selfless Ubuntu philosophy, they made a focused run through the playoffs, which triumphantly ended with them destroying my beloved Los Angeles Lakers in the NBA Finals to win the league championship (hey, not every story can have a happy ending, right?).

All joking aside—when many of the players on the 2007–2008 Celtics team reflect back on their historic run to win the NBA championship, they usually do not mention the Big Three as the primary key to their achievements. After all, there have been countless NBA teams with multiple superstars who have not found any meaningful success whatsoever. Instead, those players often credit the Celtics' universal acceptance of the Ubuntu philosophy as the key that sparked their turnaround.

You might be thinking, "That's great and all, but I don't know the difference between a slam dunk and a touchdown. How does this relate to my life in the working world?"

It relates very closely.

Regardless of whether we're talking about a professional sports team, a military unit, an elementary school, a busy restaurant, a department in a corporate office, a critical-care nursing unit, the cast of a big-budget movie, a commercial airline flight crew, a retail store in the mall, or a Silicon Valley start-up business, you will consistently notice something about those teams when they are high-functioning: *They are relentlessly focused on their collective success over individual achievement.* Whether it is on the basketball court, on the battlefield, in the operating room, on a movie set, or in the boardroom, that is what Ubuntu is all about.

Having the privilege of working with hundreds of high-functioning teams, who have embraced the "I am, because we are" philosophy, I have discovered that there are eight simple and practical strategies that they use on a daily basis that make Ubuntu come to life. I call these eight keys the "Ubuntu master plan," and I believe with every fiber of my being that when these keys are put into action consistently, it can take any team from last place to the championship in no time.

Let's begin by diving into the eight keys, and then explore how to make them the new normal on your work team.

Ubuntu Key #1: Address It

> **DEFINITION:** Conflict among team members is addressed quickly, maturely, and with appropriate transparency.

A few years ago, I consulted with a department in a large organization that was deeply mired in interpersonal drama. During my very first visit with them, they made no attempt to hide their contempt for each other. I remember walking into the large meeting space and noticing how the different cliques in the department sat together and refused to even make eye contact—much less communicate—with anyone else in the department who was not a member of their mini-tribe.

Calling this department a low-functioning team would be like telling you that water is wet—you already know that. What you may not know is *why* they were so low-functioning.

About fifteen minutes into the session, one of the employees in the room finally spoke up. With palpable passive-aggressiveness dripping off every word, she said, "There is someone in this room, who must go nameless, who I had conflict with two years ago. And even though I am forced to work in the same department as her, I will never be cordial to her or speak to her ever again. And you can't make me!"

As staggeringly immature as that was, what was worse was the response of everyone else in the room. They all nodded their heads as if to say, "Yep, that's how we deal with things around here." A telltale sign of low-functioning teams is an inability—or an unwillingness—to address conflict in a mature, direct, and respectful manner. Instead, low-functioning teams generally resort to talking *about* people instead of *to* people when it comes to addressing conflict.

This mentality does not align with the "I am, because we are" philosophy of Ubuntu. If we are all connected, what sense does it make to hold onto old grudges, slights, and resentments? As the famous quote goes, wouldn't that be like drinking poison and expecting the other person to die?

The first Ubuntu key, *Address It*, means that conflict is handled quickly and with appropriate transparency. On high-functioning teams, if something is affecting two team members' ability to work together and positively contribute to the team, it is addressed immediately. Conflict is not allowed to fester on high-functioning teams; rather, it is addressed in a professional manner, both parties are able to put the issue behind them, and, most importantly, afterward they move on together.

Ubuntu Key #2: Flex It

DEFINITION: Team members are willing to consistently step outside their designated roles to further the success of the team.

Have you ever asked a colleague on your work team to complete a task that is outside her job description? If you currently work on a low-functioning team, the response is as predictable as the sun rising in the east and setting in the west. Upon hearing your request, your colleague's eyes will widen, she will toss her head backward and curl her upper lip in disgust as if she were about to walk into a port-a-potty at the county fair, before she incredulously replies, "Um . . . that's not my job."

<Sigh> That is not my job.

Not only have those five pitiful words never been uttered by anyone who has enjoyed any measure of professional success, but that phrase is also not used on high-functioning teams who believe in the Ubuntu philosophy.

Highly functioning teams, who embrace the "I am, because we are" philosophy, realize that their primary job is to support the collective team's success in any way possible—and to do that well requires flexibility. Yes, it is important to fully understand your role on the team, but an unwillingness to adapt your approach to new circumstances and expand your role to support the team can be greatly detrimental.

Teams who have mastered the *Flex It* key are easy to spot. During a day when the department is short-staffed, the manager of one of these teams steps onto the front lines to lessen the load for his team, instead of allowing his team to become overwhelmed. The theme park executive of a team like this notices a stray candy wrapper on the ground, immediately picks it up, and disposes of it, instead of calling over someone else on her team to pick it up. The janitor on such a team notices that a patient is lost on the way to a doctor's appointment, and personally takes the time to walk him to his appointment, instead of assuming that someone else will help him.

In those cases, it may not be explicitly written in their job descriptions to do those things, but these people understand that for the team to enjoy collective success, each team member will have to be willing to go beyond their particular roles to benefit the team.

Ubuntu Key #3: Honor It

DEFINITION: Team members are recognized and appreciated for the positive contributions they make to the team.

Another line that is often uttered on low-functioning teams is this: "The only time anyone ever says anything to me around here is when I'm doing something wrong." Sadly, it is not a secret that many employees feel unappreciated, or at best, underappreciated at work in America. According to a recent study by the Achievers Corporation:

» 53% of the people surveyed don't feel recognized for their achievements at work.
» 57% of the people surveyed don't feel recognized for their progress at work.
» 60% of the people surveyed don't receive in-the-moment feedback from their managers.[1]

In many professional environments, people are always on the hunt for issues that are going wrong, in hopes of fixing those issues and optimizing results. But what happens when that single-minded pursuit comes at the expense of honoring the meaningful and positive work that is happening on a daily basis? The answer to that question appears in the bulleted statistics above.

Embracing the Ubuntu philosophy is not about ignoring the things that are falling apart in our workplaces. But while addressing those problems, it is also about steadfastly honoring the positive work that is being done to move the team closer to collective success. In the workplace, this means consciously taking the time to honor these behaviors by *personally*, *sincerely*, and *consistently* recognizing the efforts and results of your fellow team members.

It does not matter if this recognition is peer to peer, leader to employee, or employee to leader. The key is ensuring that your colleagues know that their positive contributions are making a meaningful difference to the team. Most importantly, this kind of positive reinforcement is a top priority and it is done consistently.

Ubuntu Key #4: Support It

DEFINITION: Team members are willing to act selflessly to assist other team members who are struggling.

In Chapter 2, I recounted the story of how wildlife activist Boyd Varty's life was saved by his friend and mentor Solly, who courageously waded into a crocodile-infested river to rescue him. As Boyd tells the story, Solly's decision to put himself in grave danger to help his friend was "as natural as breathing."

This is exactly how teams who embrace the Ubuntu mind-set operate as well.

Instead of having the radio station locked in on WIIFM (What's In It For Me?), high-functioning teams are consistently focused on how they can selflessly increase the team's collective success. The question that is on team members' lips most often is this: "How can I help?" And similar to the situation with Boyd, they ask this question consistently—especially when things are spiraling out of control.

In the past year, in my travels across the country as a speaker, I have heard some very tragic stories, but two of them stand out to me in particular. I met a woman whose daughter mysteriously contracted an aggressive viral infection shortly after she was dropped off for her freshman year in college, and died a few weeks later. I met another woman who was walking her beloved dog in her neighborhood one evening after work, and the dog was mauled to death by two pit bulls in front of her eyes. Besides enduring the unthinkable pain of both events, there was another thing that both of those women had in common. *They both told me that there is no way that they would have gotten through it without the support and love of their work teams.*

That is why the *Support It* key is at the heart of the Ubuntu philosophy. Team members on these high-functioning teams help without judgment, and consistently show their support by alleviating the suffering of colleagues.

To them, it is as natural as breathing.

Ubuntu Key #5: Live It

> **DEFINITION:** Team members' habitual way of thinking is positive and solution-oriented.

One thing that you almost always see on low-functioning teams is team members with attitude problems. You know the ones I'm talking about—they do the least amount of work they can to avoid being fired, they complain incessantly without providing solutions, they treat their colleagues and customers horribly, and, worst of all, they have no interest in changing or intention to change. I am willing to guess that those behaviors are not listed on any organization's core values list.

The *Live It* key is about doing the exact opposite of all of that. On high-functioning teams, team members know the core values of their organization or work team, and instead of merely posting them on a bulletin board somewhere, they actually *live out* those core values on a daily basis. As Mahatma Gandhi would say, this is about being the change that you want to see in the world—or, in this case, on your work team.

High-functioning teams who perform this key well have a relentlessly positive attitude. And, no, a positive attitude does not mean that you will smile happily if you just found out that half your work team is going to be laid off. As I have said before, there is nothing positive about delusion. A positive attitude is about the critical choice not to stay stuck in the inevitable problems of the workplace, and choosing to focus on potential solutions instead.

Teams who choose the Ubuntu philosophy consistently think, behave, and work in ways that are aligned with the team's highest core values.

They know that by living those traits, the team's collective success is all but guaranteed.

Ubuntu Key #6: Own It

DEFINITION: Team members have high levels of self-accountability by choosing to own instead of choosing to blame.

"It's my coworker's fault."

"If the organization would just pay us more, we wouldn't do such a mediocre job."

"I can't do that because no one took the time to train me."

These are the common, soul-draining examples of statements from people on low-functioning teams. Anyone who cares about the collective success of the team does not have the luxury to wallow in these types of defeatist thoughts.

High-functioning teams focused on the Ubuntu philosophy are all about accountability and taking ownership—especially when problems arise, balls are dropped, and things start falling apart. While low-functioning teams are slinging around blame and making excuses, high-functioning, Ubuntu-powered teams are making the wiser choice. In the Ubuntu mind-set of "I am, because we are," blaming others is the same as blaming yourself. So, instead, when things inevitably go wrong, high-functioning team members look within and ask themselves, "What part of this situation do I own?" or "How did I contribute to this problem in some way?" This creates an environment of accountability.

In fact, it is not uncommon on high-functioning teams to battle (I am using that term loosely) over *who owns more of a problem*. For example, if a deadline for a task is not met, you may see one high-functioning team member say, "I should have paid closer attention to the project time line to see if we were on track to complete it on time." Upon hearing that, another team member may add, "I also should have checked in with you to see if you needed assistance, and I didn't do that. And I apologize." The manager may even chime in and say, "I should have ensured that the project time lines were communicated more clearly, and I'm sorry that I didn't do that."

You might be rolling your eyes so hard that they are firmly in the back of your head at this point, but if you are, isn't that proof of how unaccountable most of our work cultures currently are? The reality is that high-functioning teams who fiercely *Own It* are far more prevalent than you may imagine, but we are so accustomed to dealing with the opposite that we cannot even believe in their existence.

Like most things, it does not have to be that way, but that is only possible if we are willing to own our part of the problem.

Ubuntu Key #7: Protect It

> **DEFINITION:** Team members are dedicated to ensuring the personal, professional, and psychological safety of all team members.

Have you ever sat in a business meeting and privately wondered what in the world everyone was talking about? I know I have. More troubling, however, is the fear to raise your hand to ask for clarification. This is all too common in organizations throughout America.

On low-functioning teams, you will rarely see team members stand up and say, "I don't know" or "I need help" or "I'm burned out." Instead, these low-functioning team members do something that is far more destructive. They lie and pretend that they have it all figured out so they can save face, which accomplishes nothing besides creating additional problems on top of the original ones.

High-functioning teams, who believe in the Ubuntu mind-set, do the opposite by protecting the team members' ability to speak the truth and safely share what is on their minds. This is often known as psychological safety, which researchers at Google determined was the most important factor in creating a highly effective team. They defined psychological safety as:

> The belief that a team is safe for risk taking in the face of being seen as ignorant, incompetent, negative, or disruptive. In a team with high psychological safety, teammates feel safe to take risks around their team members. They feel confident that no one on the team will embarrass or punish anyone else for admitting a mistake, asking a question, or offering a new idea.[2]

Coincidentally, the team at Google who conducted this research was code-named Project Aristotle, in honor of his famous quote, "The whole is greater than the sum of its parts." His quote aligns nicely with the African proverb that inspired the title of this book, "If you want to go fast, go alone. If you want to go far, go together." If that is not powerful evidence that teamwork is a timeless concept, then I do not know what is.

Because Ubuntu-driven teams are deeply connected, there is no sense in shaming people for not knowing something, asking for help, or sharing new ideas—because doing so would only drive wedges between team members instead of creating connection. The goal instead is to diligently protect the safety of team members to share any thoughts that would add to the collective success of the team. This is one of the best ways to increase collaboration and trust on a work team.

An excellent example of this is morbidity and mortality (often known as M&M) conferences that are convened in hospitals when a patient dies. Doctors, nurses, and others who are involved in the case are asked to forthrightly offer their thoughts on what went wrong in a safe, confidential environment, so that the hospital can avoid similar mistakes going forward. In situations like this, the *Protect It* concept not only builds stronger teams, it can also save lives.

Ubuntu Key #8: Say It

DEFINITION: Team members consistently communicate in ways that are clear and respectful.

On low-functioning teams, members do not give meaningful attention to how they communicate with others. For example, if a team member feels that cursing out a colleague is the best way to get his point across, he would not think twice before doing it. Another example of low-functioning communication is when a team member chooses to communicate in a kind manner to a senior leader or to a customer, and then turns around and communicates with a colleague or subordinate with disrespect. Equally as bad, on low-functioning teams you will see people with no idea what they should be working on, or if they are on the right track, because of a lack of meaningful feedback.

The final Ubuntu key, *Say It*, focuses on the importance of effective communication on a work team. High-functioning teams pay a great deal of attention to how they communicate with each other. This includes many aspects, but below are the two most important ones:

1. They communicate respectfully by avoiding yelling, name-calling, gossiping, writing emails in all capital letters, or doing anything else that shows a lack of respect for another team member.

2. They ensure that team goals are clearly communicated so that everyone knows the direction of the team, and how they are expected to contribute.

Say It is the backbone of any high-functioning team.

Putting the Keys into Action

Recently, I facilitated a very simple exercise for a group of nurses. The premise was straightforward—all I did was have each of them write down on a 3x5 index card their response to this question: "What does it mean to you to be on time for your 7:00 a.m. shift?" As I said, very simple stuff. Of course, all the responses were exactly the same, right?

Well, not exactly.

Once I received all the index cards, I read them aloud to the group. Here are some of the most memorable examples:

» Nurse #1: "Being on time for my 7:00 a.m. shifts means that I arrive at the hospital at 6:30 a.m., I grab my oatmeal with flaxseed, spend some time in quiet reflection to ensure that I'm in the right mind-set, and then I head up to the unit at 7:00 a.m., ready to work."

» Nurse #2: "As long as I'm pulling into the parking garage of the hospital at 7:00 a.m., I'm on time."

» Nurse #3: "If I'm pulling out of the driveway of my apartment building at 7:00 a.m. I'm on time, because my commute time should be paid for by the organization."

This exercise should be *very* concerning to you. Sticking with this example, what a lot of leaders do during their team meetings is simply say, "I need everyone to be on time for their 7:00 a.m. shift." And the employees hear that and think, "Got it, boss!" as they go back to doing *whatever they believe that means.*

Specificity is the key to making the Ubuntu master plan work. So, how do we get this specificity? We must ask our work team to create it.

For example, let's say that your team wanted to increase accountability (Key #6: *Own It*). During a team meeting, you can simply post the definition of *Own It* ("Team members have high levels of self-accountability by choosing to own instead of choosing to blame"), and ask team members to brainstorm ideas of how they can accomplish this on their team.

Some examples may include:

» We should not expect others to do something that we are capable of doing ourselves.
» We will not make excuses or cast blame when things go wrong; instead, we will take ownership.
» We will reject any situations where we believe that we are helpless and retain our power.

The beauty of this simple exercise is that the ideas to put the *Own It* key into action are not being forced on the team; *they are being created by the team.* This makes it easier for team members to enforce those ideas when they fall short of the agreed-upon team standards. Shared norms enable teams to effectively go together; without them, team cohesion and the spirit of Ubuntu become impossibilities.

Creating high-functioning teams does not happen by chance. It requires attention, dedication, and, most of all, a plan. With Ubuntu as your true north, it becomes easier to create teams that are more focused on collective success than individual performance.

CHAPTER 9

Your Power Is Not for Sale: Dealing with Enemies of Ubuntu

The most common way that people give up their power is by thinking they don't have any.

—Alice Walker

The entire book up to this point has been all about the importance of connection, the power of Ubuntu, and the willingness to go together. While that is all true, it would be naive not to discuss the challenge of working with people we would prefer not to connect with in any way (and those who would prefer not to connect with us, for whatever reason).

Despite our best efforts and intentions, we will still encounter difficult personalities in the workplace, and outside it as well. My hope is to share how we can still stay true to the Ubuntu mind-set, even when we are face-to-face with some of the most unpleasant colleagues imaginable.

There's a lot to cover, so let's dive in.

Your Most Critical Asset

I chose to open this chapter with the quote from Alice Walker, because it can be very easy to forget the truth of her sage words when dealing with challenging people of any kind. It can also be easy to slip into helplessness and victimization when dealing with a toxic boss or backstabbing coworkers. As true as that is, it does not change the fact that we will always remain in the driver's seat when we recognize our power and commit to never giving it away to another person. Your power is not for sale.

So, what does it mean to give your power away? It means that you are relinquishing to someone else the power to achieve a desired result. This becomes extremely troublesome when you give other people the keys to control how you feel. If your desired result is to feel at peace, but you allow your boss or colleagues to make you feel bitter, inadequate, furious, sad, or miserable, you have effectively given your power away. Rule number one of dealing with difficult people is that *you should never give them the power to control how you feel.*

Easier said than done, isn't it? Yes, definitely. But just like every new skill you have learned and will learn for the rest of your life, it is always hard before it becomes easy. Maintaining your power is certainly one of those skills that will be hard at first. On a positive note, practice and steadfast attention to this all-important skill will make the difference between successfully dealing with these folks or allowing them to control your happiness and your sanity.

Your power is yours and yours alone. It is not for sale, and you certainly are not going to give it away for free, either. Following are some best practices to always maintain your power.

....

Between stimulus and response there is a space. In that

space is our power to choose our response. In our response

lies our growth and our freedom.

—*Viktor Frankl*

....

Focus on What You Can Control

When people focus on external elements outside their control to make them happy, it is a predictable recipe for misery. If you are waiting to be happy when your colleague stops having loud cell-phone conversations in the neighboring cubicle, when you get the big raise, when you get the promotion that you feel you deserve, when you are finally able to change your work hours, or when your boss stops acting like a narcissistic diva, you might be waiting for a long time.

Worse still, since you are not in direct control of any of those things, you have effectively given your power away to the external forces that may not find it as urgent a priority as you do. Instead, shift your focus to the only three things that you will be able to control until the day that you die.

1. Your actions

Regardless of what is going on around you, you will always have complete control over your actions and reactions. The quote from Viktor Frankl, cited above, holds the secret to remaining in possession of our power. In that tiny space between stimulus and response, we get to decide who will own our power: *them or us*. This is the action that we always get to control.

When your colleague passive-aggressively comments about how your presentation at yesterday's all-staff meeting was "all over the place," you are presented with an opportunity to show the world what you are all about. The space between stimulus and response is in your possession and it is your move. What are you going to do?

If you have committed to not giving your power away, you do not have to take her bait when you are in that space. Instead, you can look her in the eye and say, "Thanks for the feedback" or "I'm sorry you felt that way about my presentation—do you have any specific suggestions about how I can improve?" (Obviously, if you don't care about her opinion, feel free to skip the second suggestion.)

The point is that your actions can always be aligned with the highest version of yourself. Even if she is someone you would never want to connect with, you can still behave in a way that exemplifies the Ubuntu philosophy. Sometimes the most positive action you can take is to drastically limit your interaction with toxic colleagues. Instead of seeking a deeper in-person connection, as recommended earlier in this book, you can send them love and kindness from a distance that is as far away from them as humanly possible.

2. Your effort

When dealing with difficult people, especially at work, it is not uncommon for us to give less than our best effort. Again, if we allow that to happen, we have effectively given our power away to those people to negatively affect our lives, which is not an ideal way to maintain our productivity, sanity, and happiness.

Your actions are what you do, but your effort refers to *how hard you do it*—and, similar to your actions, this is also always under your control. You can choose the right actions, but if you abandon them once you are faced with a challenging situation, that is proof that you are not committed. Effort is about commitment, and this is the hard part of maintaining your power. When you are dealing with a toxic colleague or boss, you continue to own your power by not lowering yourself to behave in the same manner that he does.

And, yes, this requires a great deal of commitment and effort, but the payoff of maintaining your power will make it worthwhile.

3. Your attitude

I saved the most important one for last. Your attitude, which is your habitual way of thinking, is also fully within your control—and it is one of the best weapons at your disposal for dealing with toxic colleagues.

As covered in Chapter 2, it helps to maintain our curiosity when dealing with behavior that we don't understand. Rude customers, self-preservationist colleagues, or narcissistic bosses can be exhausting to deal with, but if we are able to shift our attitude toward them to a place of curiosity rather than judgment, we will be able to remain in control.

The one mental trick I use to keep my attitude in check when dealing with toxic people at work is to remember that *hurt people hurt others.* These days when I'm dealing with a hate-filled person of any kind, I don't see her as the intimidating persona that she is trying to portray. Instead, I see her for who she is: a person who is riddled with fear and pain, and does not know how to deal with it except by being a jerk to others.

In the Ubuntu philosophy of "I am, because we are," it makes no sense to have habitual thoughts wishing others harm or ill fortune. My thoughts belong to me, and I have no interest in giving a toxic person the power to fill my thoughts with negativity and my life with stress. I don't have to hug a toxic colleague and I certainly do not have to like him, either.

What we cannot do is allow these people to alter our thoughts and lower our faith in the goodness of humanity.

> *The more concerned we become over the things we can't*
>
> *control, the less we will do with the things we can control.*
>
> —John Wooden

Do More of What They Hate

In one of my previous jobs, I was stuck in a toxic workplace where I was treated horribly on a daily basis for doing something inexcusable: *smiling too much*. Yes, you read that correctly.

According to what I found out after I quit that job, my former colleagues would take bets on who would get me to break first. They would take my sandwich out of my lunch bag, stomp on it so that there was a visible footprint on the bread, and then put it back in my bag. They would give the angriest customers my direct telephone line so that whenever my phone rang, I would be greeted by someone loudly cursing in my ear. They even tried to modify my time card multiple times to make it appear that I was taking two-hour lunches, so that I would get in trouble with the boss. It was a miserable experience, to put it mildly.

However, I was determined not to let these people get the better of me. Since they were cowards and did those things so that it was impossible to prove who among them was the culprit, I couldn't confront them because they would deny everything. So I did the next best thing instead.

I did more of what they hated.

In other words, I kept smiling, I kept working my tail off, and I eventually became the top performer in the region—all of which drove my tormentors insane. Because I let them know that they could not affect me with their actions, I was able to maintain my dignity, my results, and, most of all, my power.

Addressing the Unacceptable: Workplace Bullying

All the strategies outlined earlier in this chapter are useful and effective when dealing with difficult and rude bosses and coworkers. However, as I mentioned before, when the behavior becomes abusive—as in the case of workplace bullying—we must take a stand.

As you may know, ending workplace bullying in America has become an obsession of mine, and it was the driving force behind what inspired me to write my first book, *Making Work Work*. In the months after its release, I was bombarded with stories from workplace bullying targets that were heartbreaking, deeply disturbing, and, most of all, unacceptable in a civilized society like America. In the Ubuntu philosophy, if one of us is hurting, all of us are. My hope is that we can use our collective strength not to connect with the toxic bullies, but to connect with one another to finally rid this world of the issue that is causing so much suffering worldwide.

Workplace bullying is defined as:

> Repeated, unreasonable actions of individuals (or a group) directed toward an employee (or a group of employees), which are intended to intimidate, degrade, humiliate, or undermine; or which create a risk to the health or safety of the employee(s).[1]

According to the most recent findings from the Workplace Bullying Survey, conducted by the Workplace Bullying Institute, *sixty million Americans* are affected by workplace bullying. That is almost one in every five Americans.[2] The effects of workplace bullying are far-reaching, devastating, and, most of all, preventable. They include:

» Hypertension
» Post-traumatic stress disorder (PTSD)
» Debilitating anxiety

- » Clinical depression
- » Strokes and heart attacks
- » Migraine headaches
- » Insomnia
- » Ulcers
- » Descent into addictions, such as alcoholism or drug abuse
- » The destruction of marriages and families
- » Suicide

As noted earlier, this bulleted list is the reality for nearly 20 percent of our country's population, and millions more all over the globe. Choosing to do nothing is no longer an option. It is time to reclaim our collective power, starting now.

··

Injustice anywhere is a threat to justice everywhere.

—*Martin Luther King Jr.*

··

Calling It What It Is: A Human Rights Violation

As a country, we are better than this. If there is something preventable that is literally destroying the lives of nearly 20 percent of our population, should we simply shrug and say, "Well, at least no one is bullying *me* at work . . ."? That is *not* the way of Ubuntu. We must respond to this crisis as if it affected all of us, because, whether we know it or not, *it does affect all of us*. Dr. King's quote, that an injustice anywhere is a threat to justice everywhere, could not be any more true.

In *Making Work Work*, I provided readers with actionable strategies for anyone to overcome workplace bullying, but in this book, it is time to take this conversation one step further. For years, many people solely considered workplace bullying to be a human resources (HR) issue. Upon deeper inspection, it is time to expand our focus. Workplace bullying is still an HR issue, but not the HR you may think.

It is time for workplace bullying to be considered a *human rights issue*. According to the organization United for Human Rights:

> Human rights are based on the principle of respect for the individual. Their fundamental assumption is that each person is a moral and rational being who deserves to be treated with dignity . . . human rights are the rights to which everyone is entitled—no matter who they are or where they live—simply because they are alive.[3]

The United Nations specifies thirty inalienable rights that every human being is entitled to in the document known as the Universal Declaration of Human Rights—the world's most widely accepted document on the subject of human rights. The thirty rights in this document are universal—it does not matter if you are a man, a woman, a member of the LGBTQ community, a Christian, a Muslim, an atheist, a person with a disability, a billionaire, a person who is penniless, a white person, a brown person, an American, or a person who lives in North Korea. The thirty rights are what each of us is entitled to simply because we are alive.

Upon inspecting the document, it is clear how workplace bullying is in violation of multiple rights:

» **ARTICLE 1**: All human beings are born free and equal in dignity and rights. They are endowed with reason and conscience and should act towards one another in a spirit of brotherhood.

- » **ARTICLE 3:** Everyone has the right to life, liberty and security of person.
- » **ARTICLE 5:** No one shall be subjected to torture or to cruel, inhuman or degrading treatment or punishment.
- » **ARTICLE 23, SECTION 1:** Everyone has the right to work, to free choice of employment, to just and favorable conditions of work and to protections against unemployment.
- » **ARTICLE 24:** Everyone has the right to rest and leisure, including reasonable limitation of working hours and periodic holidays with pay.[4]

When many people think of human rights violations, they rightly think of unspeakable horrors, such as child trafficking, slavery, torture and abuse, unfair trials, or restricted freedom of thought and expression that still occur in many places all over the world. However, workplace bullying has undoubtedly earned a seat at this unholy table with the other atrocities cited above, based solely on the widespread suffering it causes. Human suffering should not be considered less valid because someone is given a paycheck to endure it.

It is long overdue for workplace bullying to be viewed with the same seriousness and attention as any other human rights violation. If there was a known human trafficker working in the office a few doors down the hallway from your office, would you be willing to look the other way as long as he was meeting the company's quarterly projections? Would it be acceptable for you to sit silently each day at work, knowing that a torturer of children was the person who signed your performance evaluation? I doubt it.

Those might seem like extreme comparisons to make to workplace bullying, but I do not think so. Yes, human trafficking and child endangerment are both, thankfully, illegal, due in large part to the irreparable and obvious harm that those human rights violations inevitably cause. Also, thankfully, people the world over are repulsed by those crimes, which makes it more socially acceptable to stand up against them. Yet, despite the irreparable, obvious, and evidence-based harm that workplace bullying is causing to the mental, emotional, and physical health of millions of Americans, workplace bullying does not generate the same universal disdain. Not only is it fully legal in the United States, but, even worse, it is still largely dismissed by many as the price of working in a grown-up world. Yes, in America, a clear human rights violation that is destroying families, eroding health, and in some cases *literally ending lives*—remains unaddressed, dismissed, and, in some workplaces, encouraged. This is not Ubuntu—it is madness.

We are better than this.

Going Together to Heal the Working World

To heal the world, we must acknowledge our critical role in making this a reality. As individuals, our power will always remain limited, but when we choose to go together, there is nothing we cannot do. As I pointed out earlier, when we focus on the three things that are consistently within our control—our actions, our effort, and our attitude—we have the power to move forward, despite the obstacles in our way.

And the obstacles are real. There are people who do not care about connection, Ubuntu, or creating a more positive world. As much as I wish that was not the case, it is. We can sit on the sidelines dreaming of a better world, or we can actively create it. I am choosing the latter, and I need you to do the same.

Let us choose to affirm humanity by addressing these atrocities. I am challenging every workplace in America to be better. Human rights violations at any workplace are unacceptable, and employers who turn a blind eye in the name of profits are not only against Ubuntu, they are against humanity.

The power is ours to change this, and we will not give it away.

PART FOUR

LEAD TOGETHER

CHAPTER 10

Kindness Is Not Weakness:
The Heart of the Ubuntu Leader

A leader's most powerful ally is his or her own example.

—John Wooden

ver since I was a little boy, I was always fascinated by leadership or, more specifically, what I would need to do to become an effective leader. It would be many years before I had a supervisor, manager, or a boss of any kind, but I was a lifelong sports fanatic, so I often looked to the sporting world to find my leadership role models. Looking back on it, that probably was not the best place for me to start.

Without question, there are many excellent leadership examples in the sporting world, but what I seemed to notice most consistently was a "Do whatever it takes to win" approach. On television, I would see star players screaming in the rookie players' faces whenever they made mistakes on the basketball court, or testosterone-fueled football coaches becoming red-faced as they angrily berated their teams during a halftime speech, or even seeing a coach pick up a folding chair and throw it across the basketball court like a frisbee when he was upset with a referee's call. What I remembered most was that after each of those incidents, many of the fans who were witnessing these tirades would look on with doe eyes and usually offer some fawning praise like this: "Now *that's* leadership."

But is it really?

Even as a teenager, seeing that type of behavior never sat well with me. Yes, of course, sometimes you need to become fired up to get your team inspired—I get that. But, if yelling, cursing, throwing chairs, and demeaning your players when they screw up are the *only* tricks in your leadership arsenal, then, at best, you are limiting your overall effectiveness (and by default, you are doing the same to the people who are stuck following you).

I always knew that there had to be more to being a leader than being a belligerent, overbearing asshat—because, if there wasn't, then I wanted nothing to do with it. I stayed hopeful that if I kept searching, I would eventually find a leader in the sporting world who was kind, respected, and wildly effective.

And then, finally, I found exactly what I was looking for.

The Wizard Who Changed Everything

When I was a teenager, I read about a man named John Wooden. John Wooden was the head basketball coach of the UCLA Bruins, and under his leadership in the 1960s and 1970s, his teams won an unprecedented ten college basketball national championships, including an unheard-of seven national championships in a row. While UCLA's thorough, decades-long thrashing of the college basketball world was certainly impressive, what struck me the most was that he did it all by being kind, respectful, and genuinely caring about the people he led on a daily basis.

He had three simple rules that he expected his players to follow consistently: "No profanity. Don't criticize a teammate. Never be late." His nickname was the Wizard of Westwood, and even though I don't think he particularly cared for that moniker, I can see why it was given to him. I, as well as millions of other fans, were mesmerized by his ability to lead others by consistently modeling the best of humanity, and confidently believing that it would inspire the people he led to do the same. He was extremely successful in that pursuit.

His thoughts on coaching and life have become legendary, and, to this day, his wisdom has inspired leaders all over the world. Here are a few examples:

» "You cannot live a perfect day without doing something for someone without the thought of repayment."
» "Be as enthusiastic about the success of others as you are about your own."
» "Every day, try to help someone who can't reciprocate your kindness."
» "You are no better than anyone else and no one is better than you."
» "I believe we are most likely to succeed when ambition is focused on noble and worthy purposes and outcomes, rather than on goals set out of selfishness."

- » "Kindness makes for much better teamwork."
- » "There is nothing stronger than gentleness."
- » "We can give without loving, but we can't love without giving. In fact, love is nothing unless we give it to someone."
- » "You can do more good by being good than any other way."
- » "Happiness begins where selfishness ends."

I certainly did not know this as a teenager, but I do now—John Wooden was my first example of what it meant to be an Ubuntu leader. The concept of "I am, because we are" is not only an effective way to live and to work, but it is a powerful leadership strategy, too.

Best of all, I am forever grateful that his example serves as a daily reminder to leaders all over the world—whether you are leading a nation or leading your family—that kindness is *not* weakness.

Yes, Being Liked As a Leader Matters

There are plenty of examples of loud-mouthed, fear-inducing, bullying leaders in the sports world, the political arena, the business world, and even in our homes. Many of those authoritarian leaders are quick to double down on this philosophy and take a hard-line, Machiavellian stance that it is better to be feared than loved as a leader. They view building meaningful relationships based on connection, compassion, respect, kindness, and empathy as unnecessary soft skills that diminish their ability to lead, instead of enhancing it. I could not disagree more with that ideology, and I firmly believe that this is the least effective way to lead others.

The data supports this, too. Jack Zenger and Joseph Folkman—two world-renowned leadership development experts and founders of the Leadership Development Consultancy, Zenger/Folkman—conducted a fascinating study on the topic of leadership likability. Specifically, they studied 51,836 leaders and only found 27 of those leaders who were rated at the bottom quartile in terms of likability, but also in the top quartile in terms of overall leadership effectiveness.[1] Mathematically, that gives an unlikable leader about a 1-in-2,000 chance of reaching the height of leadership effectiveness. Those are daunting odds.

In my professional experience working with leaders from a wide range of industries, these are the traits that I have observed most often in likable leaders (and how they were often described by those who followed them):

» They are approachable.
» They are down-to-earth.
» They are kind.
» They genuinely care about you as a person (not just what you can do for them).
» They consistently communicate to others with respect.
» They treat you as an equal.
» They have integrity and they keep their word.
» They are willing to be vulnerable.
» They don't take themselves too seriously.
» They are consistently looking for ways to help others.
» They are competent (yes, it's hard to be likable as a leader if you don't know what you're doing).

It makes sense that anyone who chooses to be an Ubuntu leader would find that being well-liked would be a worthy pursuit. However, before you get the wrong idea about what it means to be a likable leader, let me be clear. **There is an enormous difference between *wanting* to be liked as a leader and *needing* to be liked as a leader.**

Leaders who *want to be liked* genuinely care about how their behavior and actions affect others, and they strive to create meaningful connections with them. Their primary objective is to build trust, which is the core of what it means to be an Ubuntu leader. Conversely, leaders who *need to be liked* are willing to sacrifice their dignity, integrity, values, and self-respect in hopes of being universally liked. Leaders who need to be liked are far less concerned about creating connection or building trust. Instead, their primary objective is to soothe their deep insecurities by doing whatever it takes to ensure that everyone likes them. That includes avoiding difficult conversations, failing to enforce rules, or turning a blind eye to inappropriate behavior of team members that is negatively affecting the team. The sad truth is that the leader who needs to be liked does not really care about the other person—she cares primarily about herself and using those who follow her to validate her broken self-worth. This is not Ubuntu. An Ubuntu leader wants to be liked, but she does not need to be.

The Ubuntu leader fully understands that needing to be universally liked is a fool's pursuit. When I think of the people I would consider to be Ubuntu leaders—Coach John Wooden, Martin Luther King Jr., Mahatma Gandhi, Mother Teresa, and even Jesus—do you know what they all had in common? *They had people who did not like them.* A lot of people in some cases. If those luminaries could not achieve the impossible goal of becoming universally liked leaders, what hope is there for you and me to do it? Thankfully, they were not driven by the need to be universally liked. Instead, they acted in a likable manner while staying true to their goals of helping humanity move forward. This is something we can do, and should do, every day of our lives as leaders.

When It's Cold Outside, It's Time to Bring the Warmth

The beauty of becoming an Ubuntu leader who embraces the "I am, because we are" philosophy is that you do not have to wait until you have a formal position of authority before assuming this role. If you have the ability to inspire positive actions in others to reach a desired goal and collective success, then you are an Ubuntu leader.

One of the characteristics that is most helpful in creating an environment of connection is the concept of warmth as a leader. Warm leaders sincerely make other people feel cared for, important, and accepted. They build trust easily, because they are genuinely interested in the people they are entrusted to lead, and they consistently show it through their words and actions. On the other hand, leaders who lack warmth—whether consciously or unconsciously—speak and act in ways that undermine trust and connection. When you think of the leader who has had the largest positive impact on your life, I would be willing to bet that he used his warmth to make you feel cared for, important, and accepted.

Whether you are already warm, or if you wish to cultivate more warmth as a leader, here are four ways you can do it:

1. Communicate that you care.

Shortly after I graduated from college, I worked for a very intimidating man named Jack who had no interest in creating connections with his staff. He was cold, aloof, impersonal, and made a point of keeping his employees at arm's length. He did not even know all our names (nor did he care to learn them), and he would consistently walk past members of our team without acknowledging our existence. No one on our work team liked or trusted him, and his leadership style affected how the team members interacted with each other and the customers.

In our excruciatingly awkward, biweekly, one-on-one meetings, he would consistently end his meetings with the phrase, "Do you have any feedback for me?" On the surface, that sounds like an excellent question for a leader to ask a subordinate (and it was), but if you were there to hear *how* he said it, you would quickly see that there was nothing excellent about it at all. Every time he asked that question, he would lean back in his chair, cross his arms, narrow his eyes, put a look on his face as if I had just passed gas in his office. It was almost as if to say, "You'd better not say a damn thing, son, or there will be hell to pay." Every time, my answer to his obviously insincere question was an equally insincere no.

You may be thinking that Jack was woefully lacking in self-awareness and that he desperately needed the feedback that my colleagues and I failed to give him—and you would be correct on both counts. But that is exactly my point. Jack is a perfect example of how a lack of warmth can create barriers to honest and direct communication.

Thankfully, you do not have to follow Jack's example. Simply by communicating in ways that show you care will help you project warmth and build trust in almost any interpersonal interaction. Here are some straightforward suggestions, when followed sincerely, that can help you do that:

> » Say hello to your colleagues and address them by name.
> » Be mindful of your resting face (aka, the face that you have when you are not speaking) and make sure that you are not unconsciously frowning or scowling.
> » Actively listen and use nonverbal communication to show that you are paying attention (sitting up straight, nodding to show acknowledgment, making consistent eye contact, and the like).
> » Smile with sincerity.
> » Display open body language that is welcoming, friendly, and shows a genuine interest in the other person.

Please do not make the widespread mistake of dismissing this as common sense. Look around your workplace, take a walk around town, or turn on the news, and then ask yourself—how "common" is this behavior, really? Projecting warmth may seem painfully obvious, but this is not about simply knowing the right thing to do. As always, this is about execution.

2. Keep it real.
This might be hard to hear, but you really do not know it all. Neither do I, by the way—no one does. So why do so many leaders feel the need

to pretend that they have it all together, possess unshakable confidence in their ability to handle all situations, and know the answers to every complex problem? From my observations, it is because they have been told that is what real leaders do.

Yet that is *not* leadership. If anything, behaving as if you were infallible only accomplishes three things: It creates barriers between you and others, it makes you look like an insecure fraud who is trying too hard, and, most importantly, it erodes trust and connection. Pretending that you have it all figured out as a leader, in hopes of gaining respect from others, will only succeed in doing the opposite. The people you lead are not dumb, and it is worth remembering this at all times.

Leaders who project warmth think and act in an entirely different way. They lead in a way that affirms their imperfect humanity instead of masking it, and they have the confidence to act in a way that some leaders would consider weak:

» They admit their flaws and openly share where they have fallen short.
» They are quick to apologize for making a mistake.
» They will tell you when they don't know something.
» They ask for help and accept it when it is offered to them.
» They share their failures in hopes that others may learn from them.

Before I wrote *Making Work Work*, I debated for months if I should share the story in my book about my suicide attempt, which was inspired by being bullied at work for years. There were many reasons I hesitated to recount this very dark period in my life in that book. For starters, very few people knew that story (including my parents), I held a respected leadership position in my job, I was a keynote speaker who spoke to large audiences about the importance of positivity at work, and I was a first-time author. The thought of appearing unstable, weak, and less than positive nearly paralyzed me.

Then it hit me. What was the alternative? Choosing to be a total phony and writing my book from the vantage point of a bulletproof, positivity superhero who has risen above the workplace challenges that are affecting millions of Americans? Besides being completely untrue, it would also dishonor the very real struggle that is effectively devastating lives all over our country and around the globe. I simply couldn't do that. If I was going to address these issues, I had to speak from a place that represented the unfiltered truth. So, here is how I opened by book:

I almost killed myself.

Little did I know it at the time, but those four words effectively changed my life. By sharing my story in a very public way in *Making Work Work*, I invited others to share their stories, too. I was able to create bonds of connection and trust with people as far away as Asia and Africa, and, invariably, they said that it was my willingness to share my struggles that made it happen. Today, I no longer run from my story. *I lead with it.*

The power of sharing your story and being authentic as a leader can have a long-lasting impact on the people you are leading. They are always watching you, so if you can keep it real with them, you will be rewarded with a team who will be willing to keep it real with you.

3. Stand up for what is right.

Recently, I was at the bank to get a cashier's check, and I saw a man at the bank teller's window who was extremely agitated about something. He was yelling and cursing at the bank teller, calling her names that are not worthy of repeating in this book, slamming his fist repeatedly on the counter, and treating the bank teller with extreme disrespect.

Based on my failure to act nine years ago, when faced with a similar situation in an electronics store (the story I shared in Chapter 3), I was ready this time to jump in and say something. But before I could do anything, something happened.

Moments later, Rachael, the bank manager, came out and calmly said to the customer, "Sir, if you continue to curse and yell at Sandra, I will contact security and have you escorted out of the building. Will you speak respectfully to Sandra so that she can help you with your issue, or do we need to end this interaction now?"

The agitated customer continued to act belligerently and, without hesitation, Rachael coolly motioned to the security officers who immediately escorted the customer out of the building. It was what happened next that I thought was masterful.

Rachael, who could clearly see that Sandra was shaken by this interaction, put her arm around Sandra and led her away from the bank teller's window and into the back of the bank. I needed to learn more, and when I made it to the window, I asked to speak with Rachael to thank her for her exceptional leadership example. Here is what she said to me:

"There is no way that I am going to allow someone to abuse my employees. I know that we are in the customer service business, but we are human beings with real feelings that can be hurt. I know what it is like to be treated poorly by abusive customers and not have my manager support me. Once I became the branch manager, I vowed to be the type of leader who had my team's back. It may sound weird, but as I watched the customer cursing out my employee for something that was completely out of her control, *I actually felt her pain*. I had to do something."

Now, *that* is what Ubuntu leadership looks like.

It may be easy to think of warm leaders as wimps or pushovers, but nothing could be further from the truth. As I said earlier, warm leaders sincerely make other people feel cared for, important, and accepted. In many cases, demonstrating that requires leaders to take a stand to support the people they lead. What Rachael did for Sandra was warmth in action, and even though I never had the chance to speak to Sandra, I'd bet she would be willing to run through a brick wall for Rachael, if asked.

4. Take the blame (and pass along the credit).

A few years ago, I attended an intensive, three-day workshop for people who wanted to take their leadership ability to the next level. The man in charge of the seminar was a well-respected leadership trainer, and, more importantly to me, he also walked the talk as a warm leader.

On the first day of the seminar, the hotel ballroom was having some severe audiovisual issues. The microphone kept making loud crackling noises, the opening video kept freezing up, and the audio was not clear at all. It was like a perfect storm of everything that you *do not* want to happen when you're giving a speech in front of a large group of people.

I am confident that it was likely someone else's job to ensure that the audiovisual equipment was running smoothly before he stepped onstage, but instead of using that as an opportunity to liberally spread the blame to his team and to the hotel employees, he owned 100 percent of the blame.

"This is totally on me, guys. I should have checked the A/V before we got started—I'm sincerely sorry. Let's take a quick fifteen-minute break while I get everything sorted out. In the meantime, use this time to connect with the good folks sitting next to you. I'll be right back!"

While everyone else in the audience was chatting with the people sitting next to them, my attention was locked in on the trainer to see what he was going to do once he got offstage. Would he start finger-pointing and screaming at the hotel staff and his team? Not at all. I was too far away from him to hear what he was saying to his team, but he maintained a smile, he was laughing, and he even gave a hug to one of the staffers. The break only lasted a little over five minutes or so before he jumped back onstage.

"Hi again! Everything is back up and running, but before we get started can we all please take a minute to give a warm round of applause to my team and to the hotel A/V crew? They are the brains of this operation and I am so thankful that they are here to help."

I know that this might seem like a small example of leadership excellence, but I do a lot of public speaking and I have interacted with thousands of leaders who would have done the opposite of what that leadership trainer did. In that situation, it would have been easy for him to shift the blame onto others for those technical glitches and take full credit once everything was up and running again. That is ego-driven leadership and it is the opposite of warmth. Leaders like this are very difficult to trust, because you know that, deep down, their priority is not you; it is solely about making sure they look good at all costs. We all know leaders who are selectively accountable—when they hit all their goals, they are leadership geniuses (and will happily tell that to anyone who is interested), but when they fall short, they lay the blame at the feet of someone else on their team. These types of people are extremely difficult to work for and even harder to respect.

Warm leaders inspire trust by publicly declaring that nothing of importance can be done alone. Success does not happen in a vacuum— in almost every situation, many people have stepped up to make your success, as a leader, a reality. Instead of taking that opportunity to strut around like a peacock, the Ubuntu leader is willing to pass the credit on to the men and women who made it happen. Since she knows that we are all connected, she intrinsically understands that the team's success is also her own.

Also, when things go wrong, as they inevitably do, it is important for the warm leader to privately use those situations as learning opportunities and to respectfully hold those responsible accountable. But, publicly, the warm leader is willing to own the blame. There is something incredibly inspiring about people who do this. Besides being courageous, it also demonstrates through actions that, as a leader, you fully support your team, even when things go awry.

The Strongest Foundation

Kindness, likability. and warmth are the three traits that form the foundation of Ubuntu leadership. Yes, there are people who view these traits as weak and ineffective, but I would like to ask those people: What is effective about leading in a way that is mean, unlikable, and cold? The world is changing, and I would argue that now, more than ever, we must have leaders who sincerely care about the people they lead. Coach John Wooden said it best:

> I worry that business leaders are more interested in material gain than they are in having the patience to build up a strong organization, and a strong organization starts with caring for their people.[2]

I agree. Now that our foundation is set, it is time to arm ourselves with a secret weapon that makes leading with Ubuntu even more effective.

CHAPTER 11

The Power of Presence: The Ubuntu Leader's Secret Weapon

Be where you are, otherwise you will miss your life.
—Buddha

O ver a decade ago, I received devastating news that left me reeling. My mom, who had not been feeling well for a few weeks, finally made a doctor's appointment to find out what was wrong. It did not take long after that initial doctor's appointment for our worst fears to be confirmed. My mom had cancer and it was very serious—stage 4 lymphoma.

Just a few months earlier, my parents had attended my wedding and my wife Amber and I were in the process of trying to have our first baby. Everything was moving along perfectly in my life until my mom's cancer diagnosis. The thought that my mom might not be around to see her grandchild was horrifying to me, and, admittedly, I struggled to make sense of everything.

Even though my mom was about to literally begin to fight for her life, the reality was that my life still had to move forward. I still had to pay rent for my apartment, I had to prepare for my first child's arrival, and I still had to go to work. At the time, I was relatively new to my job and, in the spirit of transparency, I wanted to make sure that my boss was aware of what was going on with my mom.

During my first one-on-one meeting with my boss after my mom's cancer diagnosis, I shared how scared I was about my mom's health and how challenging it was for me to be three thousand miles away from her while she was undergoing chemotherapy (I lived in Los Angeles and she lived in Massachusetts with my dad). It was not easy for me to have this vulnerable conversation with my boss, but I wanted her to know what was preoccupying most of my daily thoughts at the time. Tears were starting to trickle out of my eyes as I spoke about my mom, and less than two minutes into my story, a text message notification went off on my boss's cell phone. Without hesitation, she picked it up while I was midsentence and then, if you can believe this, she looked at her smartphone and started laughing. Yes, *laughing*.

I was so taken aback by being interrupted by her laughter that I likely failed in my attempt to mask my annoyance when I asked her, "What's so funny?"

Oblivious to my frustration, and while still looking at her cell phone, she chuckled, "Oh, it's just my husband. He's home alone with all the pets and he's trying to wrangle them all. He just took this picture and sent it to me—isn't it hilarious?"

She turned her cell phone toward me, and, unsurprisingly, I failed to find a speck of hilarity in the picture. I responded flatly as I wiped the tears from my eyes, "Yeah . . . hilarious."

Still chuckling to herself, she turned her cell phone back toward her and presumably started typing a text message back to her husband as she said (without making eye contact), "So, what were you saying again?"

With equal parts exasperation and disgust, I said, "It was nothing."

From that moment on, I realized the importance of presence and I vowed not to make anyone feel the way she made me feel on that morning.

Too Addicted to Lead

The sad truth is that we are more distracted than ever, and the information that is vying for our attention is unrelenting.

Some of these distractions include attending back-to-back meetings at work, fielding round-the-clock emails, taking our kids to playdates and sports practices, keeping up with who liked the latest story we posted on our social media networks, finding the best online shopping deals with two-day (or, in some cases, *two-hour*) shipping, swiping left or right on dating apps in search of a romantic companion, sifting through notifications on our smartphones with breaking news about the latest political melodrama, or managing constant emoji-laden text messages from everyone from our parents to our bosses. It is exhausting to think about it all, isn't it? Unfortunately, if you are waiting for a technological advance to save us from these challenges, you will find that they are not the cure for our ills; *they are likely the cause.*

Don't get me wrong, I am not anti-technology. If anything, I love using technology more than most people. What I am against is allowing technology—or anything, really—to erode real, meaningful connections with our fellow humans. If you own a smartphone, chances are you have struggled with this at one point or another. If so, the following statistics should be cause for extreme concern:

» The average person checks a cell phone 110 times a day.
» 61% of people sleep with their phones turned on under a pillow or next to their bed.
» 75% of users admit that they have texted while driving (additionally, 26% of car accidents are caused by phone usage).
» 12% of adults use their cell phones in the shower.
» 20% of people between the ages of eighteen and thirty-four have used their smartphones during sex.[1]

If we cannot sleep, drive a car, take a shower, or even have intimate relations without looking at our cell phones, then I would argue that we are not dealing with mere distractions. We are in full-on addiction territory, and if we are unable to overcome it, then we have no chance to lead with the spirit of Ubuntu.

Joe Kraus, a partner at Google Ventures, gave a powerful talk about how these distractions are destroying our ability to connect with others. It was called "SlowTech," and in the talk, he argued two key points that I fully agree with:

1. We are creating and encouraging a culture of distraction where we are increasingly disconnected from the people and events around us and increasingly unable to engage in long-form thinking. People now feel anxious when their brains are unstimulated.

2. We are losing some very important things by doing this. We threaten the key ingredients behind creativity and insight by filling up all our "gap" time with stimulation. And we inhibit real human connection when we prioritize our phones over the people right in front of us.[2]

It is hard to argue against both these points. The next time you dine out at a restaurant, take a look around. Chances are you will see a family where Mom, Dad, the elementary school-aged kid, and, in some cases, the toddler, are all staring at their devices without speaking to each other. Take a look around in your next business meeting, too: How many of the attendees are able to make it through the hour without using their cell phones for a purpose unrelated to the meeting? If you heard an alert notification tone on your cell phone right now, could you wait thirty minutes before looking to see what it was trying to tell you, instead of reflexively checking it immediately? Who is really in control here—the technology or us? The struggle is real.

Perhaps you think that technology is training us to become better multitaskers. And, if we are able to become proficient in managing the influx of information while we are simultaneously playing with our kids, having dinner with our friends, or having sex with our significant other, we have reached the peak of efficiency.

During "Slow Tech," Joe Kraus argued differently:

> . . . my favorite part about multitasking is that it's proven that the more you do it, the worse you are at it. Check that out. It's one of the only things where the more you practice it, the worse you get at it. The reason why that's the case is that when you practice distraction (which is what multitasking really is—paying attention to something that distracted you from what you were originally paying attention to), you're training your brain. You're training your brain to pay attention to distracting things. The more you train your brain to

pay attention to distractions, the more you get distracted and the less able you are to even focus for brief periods of time on the two or three things you were trying to get done in your multitasking in the first place.[3]

Seriously, read the brilliance in that paragraph again. I can't speak for you, but his words hit me like an avalanche of boulders when I heard them for the first time. As our addiction to these constant distractions gains a deeper and stronger hold over humanity, our ability to meaningfully connect with others at a human level becomes perilously threatened.

And as a leader with the Ubuntu mind-set, you cannot let that happen.

The Game-Changing Leadership Ability

Two weeks before writing this chapter, I decided to do something that I have never attempted in my forty-three years on this earth: I jumped out of a perfectly working airplane and went skydiving.

There is something fascinating about falling toward the earth at terminal velocity. I can promise you that I was not thinking about my high-stakes conference call the next day, what I was going to have for lunch later on that morning, whether or not people were going to like this book once it was published, or the strange squeaking noise that my car brakes were making during the drive to the airfield.

None of those things crossed my mind. Instead, *I was fiercely present in the moment.*

It was beautiful, rejuvenating, and most of all life-affirming. For a few short minutes, my attention was focused like a surgical laser on what was happening in the present moment, and it was a spiritual experience for me. Once my feet hit the ground, I breathlessly asked my tandem skydiving instructor to imagine what the world would be like if everyone could experience that level of presence consistently. His response?

"The world would change overnight."

I agree.

Don't worry, I'm not going to ask you to jump out of an airplane to change the world. What I am going to ask you to do is much less scary and far more effective: **Master the moment by being fully present with others.**

In a world where everyone is driven to stare at a glowing blue-lit screen every few minutes, what if you did the opposite? What would it mean for your overall effectiveness if you were fully focused in your meetings, your work, and in your relationships without scattering your energy and effectiveness by multitasking (which, as was already covered, does not work anyway)? What would it mean for those you lead, if they consistently felt heard, acknowledged, important, and that you were steadfastly present whenever you interacted with them?

I believe that the "I am, because we are" philosophy would become actualized. This is why the game-changing leadership ability, exemplified by the spirit of Ubuntu, is being able to sustain your attention in an increasingly distracted world.

Sounds simple, doesn't it? Perhaps—but I can promise you that it is not easy. While that is undoubtedly true, the rewards of inspiring others will be more than worth your efforts.

Bain & Company, one of the world's largest management consulting companies, has data to support this contention, too. Bain researchers surveyed two thousand employees and discovered thirty-three leadership attributes that are statistically significant for inspiring others. Among them were empathy, vision, humility, and focus. In their research, they discovered that the most important attribute of all is centeredness—or, worded differently, engaging the mind to be fully present.[4] Yes, simply staying in the moment with others can do more than make them feel good—it can actually inspire them, too.

But do we really need data to support the idea that when people are fully present during their interactions with you that is a good thing? I would be willing to guess that you know how it feels when someone is shaking your hand while simultaneously looking over your shoulder to find someone more interesting to talk to. I know that I have been there, and it is not pleasant.

As leaders, we must commit to using our presence to increase the quality of human connection and not decrease it.

Rebuilding Human Connection through Ubuntu

If we want to inspire the world to connect, then, as always, it will be up to you, me, and anyone else who picks up this book to model the way. If we are choosing to go together, a necessary step is to be present with others as we do so. Here are my three favorite ways that we can make this happen, starting today.

1. Create no-technology zones.

Our smartphones, laptops, and tablets seem to follow us everywhere, but to refocus our attention back to human connection, we need to create areas where they should not be allowed.

Ever since the fateful one-on-one meeting with my former boss that I chronicled earlier in this chapter, I vowed never to make the same mistake she did. In my current role leading others, I have made a point to turn off my cell-phone ringer *and* put it out of sight during one-on-one meetings with my team.

This is done for two reasons. The first is to let my team know that during our time together, they are the priority. Interrupting them to look at my phone during our dedicated meetings simply communicates that they will only keep my attention until my cell phone alerts me that there is something more important or interesting than them that requires my attention. The easy way to avoid this is to turn off the ringer and put the cell phone out of reach and out of sight. Putting your cell phone in front of you and turning it upside down, so that the screen is not immediately visible, does not cut it, either.

The second reason is that I want to prove to myself that I am in control of my technology, instead of the other way around. And if I am truly in control, then that means I should be fine without using it from time to time. Our minds like to play devious tricks on us by convincing us that if we don't have access to our phones for an hour or more, there will be a major emergency at work or home that we will miss. Your child will get into an accident at school, and he will be helplessly crying out in pain as all of the school nurse's phone calls go straight to your voice mail. There will be a surprise audit happening at your hospital and the CEO will angrily blow up your phone with hateful text messages in hopes of finding the location of files that only you can access.

Doubtful.

You can safely turn off your phone for an hour, and on the off chance that an emergency occurs during that time, I can promise you that if people *really* need to get hold of you, they will figure out a way to do so. I often have to remind myself that there was a time in the not-so-distant past where cell phones, emails, and text messages did not exist, and we all seemed to manage just fine.

No-technology zones extend far past one-on-one work meetings, too. As the unquestioned leader of my family, my wife Amber has instituted a no-screen rule at the dinner table (and, yes, my behavior was the reason the rule was instituted), and it has made a big difference in the quality of conversation and connection in our family.

In areas of your life where you want to lead in a way that inspires connection, commit to not allowing technology, or anything else, to get in the way of making it happen.

2. Take an extended technology detox.

Each year between the week of Christmas and New Year's, I take a week to completely unplug from technology. I do not check or respond to emails or texts (I will accept phone calls, though), I don't post on social media, and I don't work on any projects. For one week, it is solely about real, human interaction. This has consistently been one of my favorite and most rewarding weeks of the year, and I plan on doing it more often than one week this year.

When I tried this for the first time four years ago, I was initially surprised—and disturbed—by how hard it was for me to do. I remember meeting one of my friends for lunch in Los Angeles during my no-technology week, and she arrived fifteen minutes after our scheduled meeting time, due to bad traffic. For those fifteen agonizingly long minutes, when I was at the restaurant waiting for her, I had no idea what to do with myself. Normally, I would be swiping through my phone, getting caught up on basketball or football scores, surfing through social media, answering emails or texts, or playing my favorite cell-phone game to pass the time, but I purposely left my phone in my car so I would not be tempted to break my detox.

So, after reading the front and back of the lunch menu approximately 243 times, I felt my anxiety rising. I felt like an addict suffering from withdrawal symptoms, and only a quick fix from the soft blue light of my cell phone would make the discomfort go away. That was when I realized that I needed this time away from technology more than I initially thought.

I gently reminded myself that the goal of the detox was to connect with other people, so when the waitress came by to refill my water, I simply asked her how she was doing. She instantly stopped pouring my water, smiled at me, and said, "You know, that is the first time that anyone has asked me that today. I'm doing great. Thanks for asking."

We ended up having a very nice chat and, coincidentally, I found out that she grew up in the town next to my hometown of Amherst, Massachusetts (Northampton, Massachusetts). Most importantly, it reminded me that human connection is so much more satisfying than reading a box score, checking my social media likes, or reducing the list of unread emails in my inbox.

If you are up to it, I am challenging you to try a technology detox. If a week is too extreme, just try it one night after work, or during a day on the weekend. Besides being incredibly calming (once you get past the initial withdrawal, of course) and cleansing, you might even discover that you will feel freer, too.

As a leader, you need all those things.

3. Practice mindfulness.

Technology aside for a moment, one of the most powerful ways we can connect to others is by committing to deepen our connection to ourselves. It is worth remembering that before we can effectively lead others, we must start by leading ourselves. The practice of mindfulness is an excellent way to begin that process.

Merriam-Webster defines mindfulness as "the practice of maintaining a nonjudgmental state of heightened or complete awareness of one's thoughts, emotions, or experiences on a moment-to-moment basis." For leaders of any kind, I cannot think of a skill that is worth developing more than this one.

In the book *Mindful Leadership: The 9 Ways to Self-Awareness, Transforming Yourself, and Inspiring Others*, author Maria Gonzalez shares the numerous benefits of mindfulness for leaders:

» Greater focus and concentration
» Improved time management
» Improved judgment and decision making
» An enhanced ability to anticipate and serve stakeholder needs
» An increased ability to deal with conflict
» Enhanced team effectiveness

- » Greater innovation and inspiration
- » Greater productivity
- » Increased ability to deal effectively with stress[5]

There are numerous ways to strengthen your mindfulness muscles, but if you are ready to start now, begin by noticing what you are currently perceiving with your five senses. Right now, without judgment, ask yourself: What sounds do you hear around you? Put down the book for a moment and look around you. What do you see? If you are eating something right now, can you identify the flavors that you are tasting? What do you currently smell and taste right now? If those questions seem bizarre to you, I completely understand—I felt the same way when I asked myself the same questions for the first time. Now I use these questions multiple times a day as my reminder to stay mindful and gently redirect my mind back to the present moment. In a world that unceasingly is trying to rip us away from the present moment, and one where we spend so much of our time obsessing about the past and fearing the future, I believe that the practice of mindfulness is the key to reversing this trend.

And this trend must be reversed, because leading from a weakened state of mindlessness, unconsciousness, and disconnection from the current reality is not going to solve anything. Mastering the present moment by being *here now* is where your fullest power as an Ubuntu leader resides, because everything that matters—and ever will matter—is happening now.

You can only experience the undeniable truth of choosing love over fear, now.

You can only experience the pure joy of connection by being kind and warm to another person, now.

You can only experience the incomparable strength of leading with the "I am, because we are" philosophy, now.

As an Ubuntu leader, these are the things that I want you to experience, and, ideally, so much more. The key is that you need to be present in order to do so. Ironically, if I had the ability to leave the present moment and travel back in time to my one-on-one meeting with my former boss, that is exactly what I would tell her.

I did not need her to cure my mother's cancer or to offer any other miracle solutions. All that I needed was for her to be present.

In that moment, that level of connection would have given me everything that I needed.

CHAPTER 12

When You Feel Like
You Can't Continue:
The Necessity of Resilience

Every time you were convinced you couldn't go on, you did.

—Anonymous

My friend Allen took a long sip of his beer before he slumped down in his seat and defeatedly sighed, "I'm done, man. I give up. The world is officially circling the drain and there's nothing we can do about it. It sucks to be helpless as everything that I value is coming to an end."

I am sure that when he reads this, he will admit that he was being a little overdramatic, but it certainly did not feel that way at the time. Due to a brutal streak of less-than-positive stories that had hit the national news cycle at the time, Allen and I decided to meet up at the local bar and drown our sorrows. The two of us were getting together in early 2017, and I always loved my time with him because he is one of the most positive and optimistic people I know. However, that evening was not one of his better days.

Allen took another long swig of his beer and emptied his glass as he motioned to the bartender for a refill. He then looked at me and said, "You're Mr. Positivity—Mr. Making Work Work. Please tell me that you have some words of encouragement for me. What can we do to fix the mess that our world is in right now?"

He looked at me in desperate anticipation, as if the next words out of my mouth would provide the cure to cancer, the key to world peace, or, at the very least, the winning numbers in the upcoming lottery drawing. He would be disappointed by what I said next.

"Sorry, man, I don't have any answers. If things continue on like this, I think that the future will be pretty bleak, to be honest."

He slumped further in his seat. "Great. Even the most positive guy I know has given up. We're screwed . . ."

My voice strengthened in response. "Who said anything about giving up?"

He looked at me quizzically as I continued.

"Look, man, I get it—things are not great right now, but giving up is not an option. If we want to see kindness, love, and compassion make a comeback, it won't happen with us crying about it on the sidelines. I don't know what it is right now, but we have to do something. Stay down if you need to, but let's decide right now how long we will need to stay down before it's time for us to get up and take action."

I could sense Allen's energy building and the smile returning to his face as he spoke. "I knew that you would have something inspiring to say. So, how long are you going to stay down and what are you going to do once you decide to get up and take action?"

I replied, "I will stay down for as long as it takes me to finish my beer, but after that, I'm done feeling sorry for myself. Like I said, though, I don't know what to do. What I do know is that our country and our world need more unity and togetherness right now, and I will do whatever I can to help make that happen."

Allen instantly sat up in his seat as if he had sat on a thumbtack. His smile fully plastered on his face, as it normally was, he leaned forward with the answer.

"You should write a book about it."

The thought of writing a follow-up book to *Making Work Work* had been on my mind for months before our chat at the bar, but it was at that moment that I committed to writing it. And, as I noted in this book's introduction, my chance meeting with Jordan a few months afterward clarified exactly what this book would be about. The result is the book you are holding in your hands right now.

Of course, I have no idea if this book will save the world, but if that was my goal, there is no way I would have ever started it. Besides, I know that words written on a page will not save the world. That task is not up to a book—*it is up to you and me. Go Together* is my way of showing myself and the world that I am doing something to move our families, our workplaces, our communities, and our country toward a spirit of Ubuntu and togetherness.

And as an Ubuntu leader, I will need your help to do the same.

On Resilience and Digging Deep to Keep Moving Forward

I believe that all of us have moments when the going gets tough, and quitting is far more appealing than soldiering on. Whether it is staying hopeful when faced with the bleak nature of the 24/7 news cycle, continuing the long fight of turning around a toxic work culture, leaving a dysfunctional relationship, or sticking to a new workout and healthy eating plan—none of those things are fun, easy, or yield quick results.

I will put reshaping our world with the power of Ubuntu in the same category as those challenges.

As I've said numerous times throughout this book, there is nothing easy about any of this. Quitting or—equally as ineffective—leaving this work to someone else, will accomplish nothing. You are needed to keep pushing forward, even when you do not feel like it or when the path ahead does not seem clear.

This is why I saved the most important trait in our journey together for the final chapter: *resilience*. Resilience is the ability to bounce back in the face of stress, adversity, or other traumatic events. While I believe wholeheartedly in optimism, kindness, compassion, empathy, mindfulness, self-awareness, and positivity, if you were to ask me the one skill that anyone who wants to lead with a spirit of Ubuntu must possess, I'd say resilience.

One of my dear friends, whom I will call Leigh, is the epitome of a resilient leader. She is a beloved leader in her workplace, in her family, and in her community—and her inner strength is a large part of what inspires others to follow her. Despite repeatedly being on the wrong end of some extremely challenging events, she remains one of the most fiercely kind and optimistic people I have the honor of knowing. She graciously shared her story with me a few years ago on my blog, *The Positivity Solution*, and I'm going to reprint it here:

Over the course of my life, I have had a disproportionate number of horrific life experiences. Sexual molestation as a child from various people at different times, verbal and physical abuse, abandonment, bullying, death of a husband and worse things I won't mention. Any one of these things gives me a cause to be fearful, filled with hate, lack of hope, bitterness, self-pity, lack of confidence and self-loathing. But I ain't having it. The only life I know for a fact that I am guaranteed is the one I am living now, and I'll be damned if I'll let my past experiences dictate how I conduct myself in the world or steal my joy.

In a *Harvard Business Review* article, titled "How Resilience Works," writer Diane Coutu chronicled the story of man she called Claus Schmidt. Claus endured an inordinate amount of misfortune in his lifetime—events that would have understandably broken the strongest of souls. Claus had seen two of his children die from incurable diseases and a third was killed in a traffic accident, yet he consistently remained a kind and encouraging force in the news office where he worked.[1]

Harriet Tubman, the well-known abolitionist, survived unthinkable abuse as a slave, including permanent scarring from being viciously whipped and beaten by plantation owners. In one instance, when she refused to help a slave owner subdue a fellow slave, she had a two-pound weight thrown at her head with such force that she was left with seizures, severe headaches, and narcoleptic episodes for the rest of her life.[2] Yet, despite that and many other hardships, she still managed to escape from slavery, and over a period of eleven years, she successfully led more than three hundred runaway slaves to freedom.

People's stories of resilience in the face of adversity are legion. Consider prisoners of war, the enslaved, the abused, the sick and injured, and those who experienced unspeakable misfortune in their lives. I am in constant awe of their strength and their ability to persevere when there was no clear path forward. These men and women serve as my muses and inspire me when I feel that the way ahead is too hard.

How did they do it? What was their secret? How can someone like Viktor Frankl find meaning and purpose in a Nazi concentration camp, while other people are reduced to petulant toddlers when the pumpkin latte they order from the barista is five degrees cooler than they expected?

This is what we need to unpack if we are going to lead the way in making Ubuntu a mainstream concept.

The Barriers to Resilience

Before we can discover how to become more resilient, there are three toxic habits that must be destroyed completely, and without looking back. These habits erode our strength, decrease our willingness to overcome obstacles, and cripple our ability to find solutions for our problems. As you read them, think about the most resilient person you know and ask yourself if he or she engages in any of these habits.

1. Chronic complaining

Even though I dedicated an entire chapter to the hideousness of chronic complaining in *Making Work Work*, I have even more to say on the subject. To be clear, I think there are legitimate reasons to complain—many of which have already been outlined in this chapter. While that is true, my focus is on the people who, when dealing with the challenges of everyday life, choose to consistently complain instead of taking meaningful action to address those challenges. If you have an interest in leading with a spirit of Ubuntu, complaining is an indulgence that you cannot partake in often, if ever.

The main reason I want to steer people far away from complaining (aside from the fact that it is one of the most uninspiring acts a leader can do) is that it offers no meaningful long-term benefits. If you do not believe me, ask the people who have dealt with the worst that life has to offer—the unexpected death of a child, a life-shattering illness or injury, or abuse at the hands of another person. In the aftermath of those situations, every one of those people have all eventually found themselves at an inevitable fork in the road. And at that decision point, the two options become crystal clear: Either they can stay stuck in the problem by complaining to whomever will listen, or they can commit to finding a solution. History has shown us that the most resilient among us have always chosen the latter.

When I fall into the complaining trap, I often think of resilient leaders like Leigh, Claus Schmidt, Harriet Tubman, Viktor Frankl, and others who did not indulge in complaining, despite facing far more serious challenges.

If they could take positive action despite their circumstances, then, certainly, we can, too.

2. Blaming others for all your problems

The late Dr. Wayne Dyer has a great quote about blaming other people for our problems:

> All blame is a waste of time. No matter how much fault you find with another, and regardless of how much you blame him, it will not change you. The only thing blame does is to keep the focus off you when you are looking for external reasons to explain your unhappiness or frustration. You may succeed in making another feel guilty about something by blaming him, but you won't succeed in changing whatever it is about you that is making you unhappy.[3]

Who would you like to blame for your current problems? Your significant other? Your parents? Your coworkers? Your boss? Your in-laws? Your neighbor? Your sibling? Your elected official?

You might have a very real and legitimate reason to blame someone in your life for your current misfortune, and I am not writing this to minimize how you are feeling. I do want to caution you, however, that if you choose to blame others for your problems or your lack of happiness, you are effectively handing over the steering wheel of your life to those people. That extreme level of power should not be given to anyone—least of all to them.

Resilient people consistently make a different decision. They acknowledge that other people may be the source of their pain, but they refuse to let anyone else take control of their happiness, sanity, and success.

3. Making excuses as to why you can't take action

As mentioned in Chapter 9, there is no honor in giving up your power. Excuses are the easiest and most common way we do this. This is another habit that resilient people do not indulge in. Take a look at this list and let me know if you think any of these excuses are legitimate reasons not to take action:

- » Your race and/or country of origin
- » Your age (too young or too old)
- » Your weight
- » Your lack of a college degree (or not having the right degree from the right school)
- » Lack of support from your friends/family
- » You do not have any money, influence, or strategic connections
- » Your sexual orientation
- » Your hometown
- » Your preference for introversion
- » Your lack of skill, knowledge, or experience
- » The government, the economy, or because a politician you despise got voted into office

All those things may be your current reality, but resilient people do not let those things stop them from taking action. If anything, they often decide to take action *in spite of* these issues. For every single one of the items on the bulleted list above, I am confident that you likely know at least one person—probably more—who struggled with that challenge and still found success.

If so, chances are that they did not choose the helplessness of excuse making. Remember: Unless you are unconscious or dead, you are never helpless.

The Straightforward Road to Resilience

Regardless of whether you want to lead the way to reunite a family divided by interpersonal drama, heal an unhealthy work environment, or forge connections in a country that is often divided along racial, religious, and political lines, your resilience will be required.

Here are three of the most common techniques that resilient people use to keep pushing forward.

1. Remind yourself of past victories.

At the beginning of this chapter, I opened with this quote:

Every time you were convinced you couldn't go on, you did.

It's true, isn't it?

Despite every challenge that has been put in your path up to this point, you are still triumphantly here. More than simply just being here, you have likely slayed a few dragons along the way, too. So, how did you do it? Take a moment to pause and think of the most challenging moments in your life up to this point. Do you remember what you did to pull yourself out of those dark days when it seemed like survival—much less, victory—was an impossibility? That is what I want you to tap into.

Whenever I feel like I can't go on, I remind myself that I was able to pull myself back from the brink of suicide to be here now. Admittedly,

I could not have succeeded without the help of others (more on this later). But recognizing that I was able to get through that dark time is all the proof I need to show that I can survive other dark times.

As the saying goes, what does not kill us makes us stronger.

2. View challenges as opportunities.

Think of a few people you admire greatly—maybe they're family members, former teachers or mentors, or even celebrities. I would be willing to bet that part of their success, and also why you admire them, stems from their ability to overcome the challenges in their lives. On the flip side, were you ever inspired by someone who has never experienced any hardships and had everything handed to him without any effort? I doubt it.

None of us deliberately chooses to invite hardship into our life, but in many cases, resilient people look back on their adversity as a gift that helped mold them into the people they are today. As a leader, if you have overcome adversity in your life, you could also use that challenge as an opportunity to inspire others. Don't ever waste your pain.

Numerous challenges await you if you choose to bring people together at home, at work, and every place in between—that is a given. It is how you choose to view those challenges that will make the ultimate difference in whether you succeed or fail.

3. Ask for (and accept) help.

I saved the most important technique for last, and it is one that many people do not use nearly enough. When you are on the brink of drowning from overload and other people are offering to help you, are you one of those who foolishly reply, "Nope, I'm good—I got this." I know I was.

I cannot say this strongly enough: There is no honor in refusing assistance from others. Every resilient person I know has asked for help, and accepted it, at some point. Contrary to popular belief, going it alone doesn't make you a tough guy/gal to be admired; it makes you a fool who is too wrapped up in your ego to reach out for the support you need. I apologize if that sounds unnecessarily harsh, but I really need this point to hit home. Resilient people are resilient because they have the wisdom to ask for help and the maturity to accept it when it arrives.

I used to be a proud help-rejecter, and doing so almost cost me my life. Accepting help is at the heart of what it means to go together. Whether it is confiding in a family member, a trusted friend, or a colleague; seeking therapy; or calling a suicide hotline, resilient people keep moving forward because they know that they don't have to keep moving forward alone.

Where Do We Go from Here?

Before we end our journey together, I want to simply remind you of something. You have everything within you to change the world. Right now. Despite your challenges, despite how messed up you believe the world is right now, and despite your self-doubts and insecurities, you are ready. The only thing I do not know is if you have the resilience to keep pushing forward. Only you can determine that.

If you have read up to this point, there is something special about you. You envision a world that values civility, kindness, and togetherness—and, more importantly, you are willing to take action to help make it a reality. My pledge to you is that you will never be alone if you choose to take this path.

Your resilience is the key to your success. When you feel like giving up, take a moment to think about what our world could look like if you did: separateness, division, hate, fear, violence, and a lack of faith in our shared humanity as a very troubling new normal. I hope that you are as scared of that bleak reality as I am.

The good news is that we are not resigned to that fate if we can find the strength to push toward connection and togetherness. We can stand up to those who are hurting others and do something to make them stop. We can seek out those who are scared and feel alone, and remind them that we are in this together. We can show the world that love will always win out against fear. Most of all, we can light the way and lead with kindness, presence, and resilience.

All those things we can do right now, and, best of all, we can do it all together.

This book will end just as it began with these words. *If you want to go fast, go alone. If you want to go far, go together.*

We have farther to travel my friend, and, despite the distance that is still ahead of us, take comfort that you will never travel a step of it alone.

I am, because we are, and more importantly, I am *because of you.*

CONCLUSION

*Nothing ever goes away until it has
taught us what we need to know.*

—Pema Chödrön

know what I would tell them now.

I know what I would tell the boy who had his favorite jacket ripped off him so that the bullies who tormented him could urinate on it, before brutally teasing him and beating him up.

I know what I would tell the young man in his late twenties who, facing the bleak future of daily workplace toxicity, made the almost irreversible decision to end his own life.

I know what I would tell the grown man who feared that the world is too broken, too divided, too far gone to be fixed by any intervention, and chose to despondently sit it out on the sidelines.

I know what I would tell them all, because each of those people are prior iterations of me. In each of those instances, and many other instances like them, I experienced the absence of hope. When I was in those dark places, the feeling that the next day would be exactly like the one before it was both suffocating and debilitating. Perhaps you can relate. If so, here is what I would tell you with equal parts love and determination:

Go together.

When the bullies tormented me, I should have reached out to my parents or a trusted teacher for help, rather than trying to work through my fears alone. Instead, I chose to separate myself, so the pain continued.

When I believed that suicide was the answer to making all the pain go away, I should have spoken to someone—a friend, my girlfriend at the time (who is now my wife), my family members, a therapist, or the suicide hotline—instead of pushing my suffering deep into my soul. Again, I chose separateness, and, predictably, the pain continued.

When I looked around at the intensity of the division and incivility facing our country and our world, I temporarily chose to separate myself and feel helpless to do anything about it. This time, though, I made a decision to connect with the many people who are working to heal our world, and join them in the journey. Unlike the previous two versions of me, I chose togetherness over separateness in hopes of making the pain stop. In this case, it finally worked.

There is nothing meaningful that we can do alone, and as Pema Chödrön's quote at the beginning of this conclusion aptly states, until we figure out the folly of separateness, the painful lessons will continue.

And we have seen these trials repeat themselves over and over again throughout history, haven't we? These teachers have appeared to us in the form of racism, sexism, homophobia, Islamophobia, bullying and harassment, abuse, murder, sexual assault, wars, and even genocide. The question still remains: Despite the suffering that millions of people have endured by opting for separateness, what have we learned? Based on the fact that many of those challenges still remain as you read these words, I would argue that we still have much left to learn. And the timeless lesson is what the world has been trying to teach us ever since the first humans walked the earth: Our survival depends on our ability to go together.

I wrote this book with one goal in mind: I want the pain to stop. I want it to end for you, me, and everyone else who is suffering. Do I think that a book has the power to help everyone who is hurting as a result of separateness? I have no idea. One thing I know for sure is that I am not going to sit on the sidelines and leave the idea for this book unwritten inside my mind without finding out. If there is even a slight possibility that it could make a positive difference for one person, this work is worth the effort. Actually, the fact that Jordan is still alive is enough for me to know that every word I have written in this book was worth the effort.

This is my most personal writing to date, because I want you to be able to connect with me as fully as possible. By sharing my pain, my fears, and my insecurities, I hope to provide you with the assurance that it is okay to feel the same way. We do not have to be perfect—or even unbroken—to make a meaningful, positive difference in this world. The only thing we need to do to stop the recurring pattern of painful lessons from the past is to commit to going together from this point forward.

Yes, there is much work to be done, but based on the people I have met on my recent travels, I am more hopeful than ever for the future. This is not blind optimism. I have seen people from all walks of life standing up and fighting together for our shared humanity, and I have also seen that it is making a difference.

Starting today, if we commit to living together, working together, and leading together, we will positively change our world. And, always, it begins with you and me.

I appreciate you, my friend, and I honor you as we walk together on our road to healing.

Ubuntu.

ACKNOWLEDGMENTS

ohn Lennon and Yoko Ono once said, "A dream you dream alone is only a dream. A dream you dream together is reality." If my dream of creating a kinder and more connected world becomes a reality, it will be primarily due to the amazing people who have walked together with me on this journey.

To my wife Amber—there is no way that *Go Together* would ever have been written if it were not for your constant love and support for me, and for the concept behind this book. Whether it was taking care of our girls so that I could sneak away to write, picking me up off the ground (sometimes, literally) when I was debilitated by self-doubt, fatigue, or both, or simply texting me with a fist-bump emoji to remind me that I was the right person to deliver this message—I am so thankful that you were by my side for all of it. There is no place on earth I would not want to go together with you. I love you, babe.

To my daughters Kaya and Nia—every late night sitting at my computer writing this book was largely driven by the desire to leave you with a kinder world than the one you are currently living in. Although you are nine and six years old, respectively, I know without any shadow of a doubt that the two of you will play major roles in healing this world with your warmth and kindness. When that inevitably happens, I will proudly go together with you both every step of the way.

To my Mom and Dad—before I ever could believe in myself, both of you unceasingly believed in me. You never laughed at me when I said that I wanted to become an author, although many others did. You never laughed at me when I said that I wanted to create a movement to end workplace bullying in America, although many others did. And, predictably, you never laughed at me when I said that I wanted to create a more connected world in the spirit of Ubuntu. Thank you for always choosing to go together with me and my dreams, no matter how crazy they may sound.

To my brothers, Doyin and Femi—both of you are so much more than brothers to me. To me, you are my role models, my dear friends, and you are both everything that I strive to be as a father, husband, son, and citizen. I am deeply inspired by how both of you have positively changed the world, each in your own special way, and I am grateful that I am able to go together with you as we do this important work.

To my team: Argelia Monroy, Clayton Vetter, Courtney Scarlata, Debby Brown, Francesca Baldassano, Reg Randles, and Sherry Dodge—I love and appreciate you all so much. Sadly, some people may think that it's weird for me to say that, but I hope that there will be a day when more people proudly say similar things about their work teams. I wish that for just one day, reality television cameras could follow you around so that the world could see what an Ubuntu work team looks like, in action. There are no adequate superlatives to describe how I feel about you all, so I will leave it at this: Allowing me to serve as your leader has been the greatest honor of my professional life. I would go together with you into a burning building if you asked.

To Dr. Felicia Yu—whether you knew it or not at the time, I came to you for help when I was burned out, exhausted, and broken in many ways that I was not even aware of at the time. With a masterful combination of saintly kindness, clinical expertise, superhuman intuition, commitment to staying fiercely present, a disarming sense of humor, sagelike guidance, focused determination, and an incredibly down-to-earth personality— you healed me. I have worked with countless physicians in my career and as a patient, and *every single one of them* could learn from your example of clinical excellence. You are an emerald unicorn, and without you, there is no way that Go Together would have been written. If anyone is inspired by this book to go together instead of going alone, you own a large piece of that. Most importantly, when you chose to go together with me on my health journey, you literally changed my life—and possibly, many others in the process. Thank you from the bottom of my heart.

To my literary agent Frances Black, and to the amazing team at Sterling Publishing, Betsy Beier, Blanca Oliviery, Kate Zimmerman, Sari Murray, and the rest of the crew—thank you for giving me such a powerful platform to share my ideas with the world. Every day, I have to pinch myself for being in this position, and there is not a moment where I am not intensely grateful for this opportunity. I will go together with you for as long as you are willing to have me.

To the transcendent leaders who have inspired me: Brené Brown, Daymond John, Elizabeth Gilbert, E.T. (Eric Thomas) the Hip-Hop Preacher, Gary Vaynerchuk, Les Brown, Marie Forleo, Neale Donald Walsch, Oprah Winfrey, Ryan Holiday, Simon Sinek, Steven Pressfield, Tim Ferriss, Tony Robbins, and Wayne Dyer, just to name a few—thank you for your wisdom, your courage, and for allowing me to go together with you, even if it is only in my mind.

And, lastly, to Jordan—thank you for choosing to stick around. There is so much more for you to do, and it would be my honor to go together with you as you do so. You know where to find me if you need me.

NOTES

CHAPTER 1

We Can Always Do Better: The Death of Civility

1. "Civility in America VII: The State of Civility" (January 2017), https://www.webershandwick
.com/uploads/news/files/Civility_in_America_the_State_of_Civility.pdf, p. 2.

2. Ibid., pp. 3–4, 6.

3. Ibid., p. 7.

4. Ibid., p. 21.

5. Ibid., p. 10.

6. Justin Kruger and David Dunning, "Unskilled and Unaware of It: How Difficulties in
Recognizing One's Own Incompetence Lead to Inflated Self-Assessments," *Journal of
Personality and Social Psychology* 77, no. 6 (1999): 1121.

CHAPTER 2

One Word That Will Change Everything: The Invincibility of Ubuntu

1. "Ubuntu—A Lesson from the Children" (April 23, 2012), https://morvensblog.wordpress
.com/2012/04/23/ubuntu-a-lesson-from-the-children/.

2. "What Makes a Good Life? Lessons from the Longest Study on Happiness," TED talk
(November 2015), https://www.ted.com/talks/robert_waldinger_what_makes_a_good
_life_lessons_from_the_longest_study_on_happiness.

CHAPTER 4

Fear or Love: The Only Decision That Matters

1. "Marianne on Love and Fear" (February 21, 2012), https://youtube/PQ9tAwEYO4k
(0:14–0:29).

2. "Chronic Stress Puts Your Health at Risk," Mayo Clinic (April 21, 2016), https://www
.mayoclinic.org/healthy-lifestyle/stress-management/in-depth/stress/art-20046037.

3. "Cortisol: Why the 'Stress Hormone' Is Public Enemy No. 1," *Psychology Today* (January 22,
2013), https://www.psychologytoday.com/blog/the-athletes-way/201301/cortisol-why
-the-stress-hormone-is-public-enemy-no-1.

4. "What Is Love? A Philosophy of Life," *Huffington Post* (updated, December 6, 2017), https://
www.huffingtonpost.com/adrian-catron/what-is-love-a-philosophy_b_5697322.html.

5. Dr. Eva Ritvo, "The Neuroscience of Giving," *Psychology Today* (April 24, 2014), https://www.psychologytoday.com/blog/vitality/201404/the-neuroscience-giving.

When Your Beliefs Become Irrelevant: The Unpleasant Reality behind Good Intentions

1. Good Reads, https://www.goodreads.com/quotes/4504146-before-you-speak-to-me-about-your-religion-first-show.

2. Ben M. Tappin and Ryan T. McKay, "The Illusion of Moral Superiority," *Social Psychological and Personality Science* 8, issue 6 (October 19, 2016): 623.

You Belong in Any Room You Walk Into: The Importance of Healing Yourself First

1. "8 Practical Steps to Getting Over Your Impostor Syndrome," *Fast Company* (September 23, 2014), https://www.fastcompany.com/3036006/8-practical-steps-to-getting-over-your-impostor-syndrome.

Becoming the Hero: Why You Must Start Before You're Ready

1. "Top 10 Employee Engagement Statistics of 2017," OfficeVibe (July 25, 2017), https://www.officevibe.com/blog/disturbing-employee-engagement-infographic.

The Master Plan: Eight Keys to Unlocking Ubuntu at Work

1. "Getting to Greatness: The Route to Employee Engagement," Achievers Corporation (July 26, 2016), https://www.slideshare.net/Achievers/getting-to-greatness-the-route-to-employee-engagement.

2. "Identify Dynamics of Effective Teams," re:Work, https://rework.withgoogle.com/guides/understanding-team-effectiveness/steps/identify-dynamics-of-effective-teams/.

CHAPTER 9

Your Power Is Not for Sale: Dealing with Enemies of Ubuntu

1. "Workplace Bullying and Disruptive Behavior: What Everyone Needs to Know," Safety & Health Assessment and Research for Prevention Program (April 2011), www.lni.wa.gov/safety/research/files/bullying.pdf.

2. Gary Namie, PhD, "2017 WBI U.S. Workplace Bullying Survey," Workplace Bullying Institute (June 2017), http://www.workplacebullying.org/wbiresearch/wbi-2017-survey/.

3. "Human Rights Defined," United for Human Rights, http://www.humanrights.com/what-are-human-rights/.

4. Universal Declaration of Human Rights, United Nations, http://www.un.org/en/udhrbook/index.shtml.

CHAPTER 10

Kindness Is Not Weakness: The Heart of the Ubuntu Leader

1. Jack Zenger and Joseph Folkman, "I'm the Boss! Why Should I Care If You Like Me?" (May 2, 2013), https://hbr.org/2013/05/im-the-boss-why-should-i-care.

2. 80+ John Wooden Quotes on Leadership, Game and Life, http://www.quoteambition.com/john-wooden-quotes-leadership-game-life/.

CHAPTER 11

The Power of Presence: The Ubuntu Leader's Secret Weapon

1. "15 Terrifying Statistics about Cell Phone Addiction," *Daily Infographic* (May 17, 2017), http://www.dailyinfographic.com/15-terrifying-statistics-about-cell-phone-addiction.

2. Joe Kraus, "We're Creating a Culture of Distraction" (May 25, 2012), http://joekraus.com/were-creating-a-culture-of-distraction.

3. Ibid.

4. "How Leaders Inspire: Cracking the Code," Bain & Company (June 10, 2016), http://www.bain.com/publications/articles/how-leaders-inspire-cracking-the-code.aspx.

5. Maria Gonzalez, *Mindful Leadership: The 9 Ways to Self-Awareness, Transforming Yourself, and Inspiring Others* (Mississauga, Ontario, Jossey-Bass, 2012), p. 10.

CHAPTER 12

When You Feel Like You Can't Continue: The Necessity of Resilience

1. Diane Coutu, "How Resilience Works," *Harvard Business Review* (May 2002), https://hbr.org/2002/05/how-resilience-works.

2. Joseph Collins, "Harriet Tubman—Unstoppable Force for Freedom," *Infinite Fire* (February 8, 2016), http://infinitefire.org/info/harriet-tubman-unstoppable-force-freedom/.

3. 34 Inspirational Wayne Dyer Quotes (July 10, 2014), https://addicted2success.com/quotes/34-wayne-dyer-quotes-that-will-inspire-success-in-you/.

INDEX

ABOUT THE AUTHOR

Shola Richards's life's mission is an ambitious one: to end generations of professional and personal suffering simply by changing how we treat each other. Whether it is helping people to deal with soul-destroying bullying bosses, passive-aggressive family members, or toxic beliefs that place higher value on competition and separateness than on teamwork and togetherness, Shola is committed to leading the worldwide movement that will change all of it.

Shola is a dynamic keynote speaker, the best-selling author of *Making Work Work* (#1 New Release in the Workplace Culture category on Amazon.com), a workplace positivity expert, an award-winning director of training and organizational development, and a positivity writer with a passionate worldwide following. His articles have been read by people the world over, who recognize him as an authority on workplace happiness and engagement, and his work has been featured in the *Huffington Post*, *Forbes*, *Black Enterprise*, *Complete Wellbeing India*, *Business Insider Australia*, and in numerous other publications all over the world. As a keynote speaker and consultant, Shola has shared his transformative message with top universities, Silicon Valley, leading health-care organizations, and, in his greatest honor to date, as a keynote speaker for the Department of Homeland Security three days before the fifteenth anniversary of 9/11, under the Obama administration.

Last, but certainly not least, Shola is a father, husband, identical twin, and a self-professed "kindness extremist" who will not rest until bullying and incivility are extinct from the American workplace and all our communities.

You can stay updated with Shola here: www.SholaRichards.com

You can read Shola's blog here: www.ThePositivitySolution.com

You can follow Shola on social media here:

» Facebook: www.facebook.com/ThePositivitySolution.com
» Twitter: @positivitysolve
» Instagram: @positivitysolve